THE CLASSIC USDA FARMERS' BULLETIN ANTHOLOGY
ON GROWING A SMALL-SCALE CITY VEGETABLE GARDEN OR URBAN FARM

ORIGINAL TIPS AND TRADITIONAL METHODS
IN SUSTAINABLE GARDENING

BY **U.S. DEPARTMENT OF AGRICULTURE**

COLLECTS USDA FARMERS BULLETINS:
936, 1044, 818, 1733

LEGACY EDITION
CLASSIC HOMESTEADERS AND FARMERS LIBRARY
BOOK 4

Doublebit Press
Eugene, OR

New content, introduction, and annotations
Copyright © 2020 by Doublebit Press. All rights reserved.
Doublebit Press is an imprint of Eagle Nest Press
www.doublebitpress.com | Eugene, OR, USA

Original content under the public domain. Originally published by the U.S. Department of Agriculture: FB 818 The Small Vegetable Garden (1917); FB 936 The City and Suburban Vegetable Garden (1918); FB 1044 The City Home Garden (1919); 1733 Planning a Subsistence Homestead (1934)

This title, along with other Doublebit Press books including the Classic Homesteaders and Farmers Library, are available at a volume discount for youth groups, outdoors clubs, or reading groups.

Doublebit Press Legacy Edition ISBNs
Hardcover: 978-1-64389-137-8
Paperback: 978-1-64389-138-5

Disclaimer: Because of its age and historic context, this book could contain content on present-day inappropriate methods, activities, outdated medical information, unsafe chemical and mechanical processes, or culturally and racially insensitive content. Doublebit Press, or its employees, authors, and other affiliates, assume no liability for any actions performed by readers or any damages that might be related to information contained in this book. This text has been published for historical study and for personal literary enrichment toward the goal of preserving the American handcraft and outdoors recreation tradition, timeless trade skills, and traditional artisanal knowledge.

First Doublebit Press Legacy Edition Printing, 2020
Printed in the United States of America
when purchased at retail in the USA

INTRODUCTION
Classic Homesteaders and Farmers Library

The old experts of artisanal trades, country and homestead knowledge, and the woods and mountains taught timeless principles and skills for centuries. Through their timeless books, the old experts offered rich descriptions of how the world works and encouraged learning through personal experiences *by doing*. Over the last 125 years, manufacturing, farming, and construction have substantially changed. Of course, many things have gotten simpler as equipment and technology have improved. In addition, some activities of pre-digital times are now no longer in vogue, or are even outright considered inappropriate or illegal. However, despite many of the positive changes in manufacturing and crafting methods that have occurred over the years, *there are many other skills and much knowledge that have been forgotten.*

By publishing the reprint series of the old USDA *Farmers' Bulletin*, it is our goal at Doublebit Press to do what we can to preserve and share the works from forgotten teachers that form the cornerstone of the history of the American artisans and traditional crafts. So much farm, homestead, and handcraft knowledge was passed to each generation through experience and hard work. An original mission of the US Department of Agriculture was to optimize farm outputs and increase the quality of life on farms through handcrafts, construction, and old-time farm tricks, tips, and skills. In their *Farmers' Bulletin* series, the USDA captured and passed on knowledge that applied to far more than just farmers!

Through remastered reprint editions of timeless classics, perhaps we can regain some of this lost knowledge for future generations. Today's interest in mastery of old handcraft skills, homestead self-sufficiency, and artisanal character has renewed an interest in the old arts. Luckily, the USDA's *Farmers' Bulletin* series contains thousands of pamphlets dedicated to teaching, improving life, and ensuring self-sufficiency to thrive in both the city and on a farm.

This book is an important contribution traditional handcraft and country skills literature and has important historical and collector value toward preserving the American handcraft and outdoors tradition. The knowledge it holds is an invaluable reference for practicing skills and hand craft methods. Its chapters thoroughly discuss some of the essential building blocks of knowledge that are fundamental but may have been forgotten as equipment gets fancier and technology gets smarter. In short, this anthology of *Farmers' Bulletin* pamphlets was chosen for Legacy Edition printing because much of the basic skills and knowledge it contains has been forgotten or put to the wayside in trade for more modern conveniences and methods.

With technology playing a major role in everyday life, sometimes we need to take a step back in time to find those basic building blocks used for gaining mastery – the things that we have luckily not completely lost and has been recorded in books over the last two centuries. These skills aren't forgotten, they've just been shelved. *It's time to unshelve them once again and reclaim the lost knowledge of self-sufficiency.*

Based on this commitment to preserving our outdoors and handcraft artisanal heritage, we have taken great pride in publishing this book as a complete original work. We hope it is worthy of both study and collection by outdoors folk in the modern era of outdoors and traditional skills life.

Unlike many other photocopy reproductions of classic books that are common on the market, this Legacy Edition does not simply place poor photography of old texts on our pages and use error-prone optical scanning or computer-generated text. We want our work to speak for itself, and reflect the quality demanded by our customers who spend their hard-earned money. With this in mind, each Legacy Edition book that has been chosen for publication is carefully remastered from original print books, *with the Doublebit Legacy Edition printed and laid out in the exact way that it was presented at its original publication.* We provide a beautiful, memorable experience that is as true to the original text as best as possible, but with the aid of modern technology to make as beautiful a reading experience as possible for books that can be over a century old.

Because of its age and because it is presented in its original form, the book may contain misspellings, inking errors from print plates, and other printing blemishes that were common for the age. However, these are exactly the things that we feel give the book its character, which we preserved in this Legacy Edition. During digitization, we ensured that each illustration in the text was clean and sharp with the least amount of loss from being copied and digitized as possible. Full-page plate illustrations are presented as they were found, often including the extra blank page that was often behind a plate. For the covers, we use the original cover design to give the book its original feel. We are sure you'll appreciate the fine touches and attention to detail that your Legacy Edition has to offer.

For traditional handcrafters and classic artisanal enthusiasts who demand the best from their equipment, this Doublebit Press Legacy Edition reprint was made with you in mind. Both important and minor details have equally both been accounted for by our publishing staff, down to the cover, font, layout, and images. It is the goal of Doublebit Legacy Edition series to be worthy of collection in any outdoorsperson's library and that can be passed to future generations.

Every book selected to be in this series offers unique views and instruction on important skills, advice, tips, tidbits, anecdotes, stories, and experiences that will enrich the repertoire of any person who enjoys escaping a bit from today's modern technology-based, cookie-cutter, and highly industrialized skills. Instead, folks seeking to make things with their hands like the old days may find great value from these resurrected instructional manuals from the past. These books were not simply written to be shelved in a library – they contain our history and forgotten methods to make things with real character and energy with a *human* component.

Therefore, to learn the most basic building blocks of a craft leads to mastery of all its aspects. We hope this book helps you along this path with its rich descriptions and illustrations!

About the USDA Farmers' Bulletin Series

Back in the early 1900s, the US Department of Agriculture (USDA) began publication of small pamphlets that were meant to improve the outputs of America's farms, promote self-sufficiency, and help farmers and farming communities thrive. This publication series continued for decades, and volumes were always available when someone wanted to learn more about a specific skill or topic that could come in handy on the homestead.

Each of the 2,000+ volumes specializes in one specific topic, be it growing a certain crop, raising a particular animal, or building a type of farm structure. Each of the pamphlets captured the best knowledge available at that time, which often represented decades or centuries of old farmer knowledge, which we know, is incredibly useful and reliable!

As we continue to blaze paths into the digital frontier, many of these lost "farmers' tips" have become more useful than ever, particularly to folks looking to start homesteads and small-scale farms, as well as those who just want to live more sustainably, simply, and consciously in light of today's factory processed world. The *Farmers' Bulletin* is also highly useful for people who live in cities, as they contain much information for community gardens, urban and rooftop farming, and sustainable living tips.

Unfortunately, many of these print volumes of the *Farmers' Bulletin* are now out of print. Indeed, because these texts are in the public domain, they are easily found and are available on the Internet. However, many of these books that are easily found on the web are often low-resolution photocopies, complete with scribble marks or other distracting spots. For the first time, high-quality, professionally restored *Farmers' Bulletin* reissues are being made by Doublebit Press to increase access to the timeless knowledge that each contains.

This Doublebit Press Legacy Edition republishes this tradition of handcrafted quality and artisanal work. We hope that this deluxe printed edition of this book will help you gain mastery in your craft, as it is presented in the exact form that it was originally published. Even today, the knowledge contained within its pages are timeless and have much to teach!

Finally, as works of art, the USDA *Farmers' Bulletin* issues contain beautiful illustrations and line art that are a sign of simpler, yet authentic times when quality mattered and craftsmanship was king. This collectible volume makes a great addition to the bookshelf of any handcrafter, maker, artisan, farmer, homesteader, or outdoors enthusiast!

Enjoy some old-time, vintage charm when the government actually encouraged you to be self-sufficient with these beautifully illustrated and classic instruction manuals by the USDA!

THE CITY AND SUBURBAN VEGETABLE GARDEN

H. M. CONOLLY
Assistant Horticulturist in Agricultural Education

A Typical City Garden

FARMERS' BULLETIN 936
UNITED STATES DEPARTMENT OF AGRICULTURE

Contribution from the Bureau of Plant Industry
WM. A. TAYLOR, Chief

and the

States Relations Service
A. C. TRUE, Chief

Washington, D. C.   February, 1918

Show this bulletin to a neighbor. Additional copies may be obtained free from the Division of Publications, United States Department of Agriculture

THIS BULLETIN is intended primarily to show the importance of gardening in city and suburban districts and to encourage greater efforts in these sections.

City gardening in back yards and vacant lots may be made the source of considerable profit and furnishes healthful exercise for the members of the family.

Gardening under the conditions that exist in cities and towns is essentially different from gardening in the country, in that city people as a rule are not experienced in the art of growing plants.

Proper organization and instruction are essential to get the most out of city gardening. In the following pages suggestions are given for conducting the work of organization, as well as directions covering the preparation of the soil, the starting of plants, and the cultivation and care of all the more important garden crops.

THE CITY AND SUBURBAN VEGETABLE GARDEN.

CONTENTS.

	Page.		Page.
Importance of city gardens	3	Plants	17
Types of gardening	5	Hotbeds and cold frames	18
Cost and value of crops from home gardens	7	Fertilizing the garden	22
Labor and expense required to make home gardens	8	Liming	24
		Preparing the soil	25
Location and soil	10	Time of planting	28
Size of the garden	12	Setting plants	31
Arrangement of the garden	12	Cultivation	32
Fences and windbreaks	14	Irrigation	33
Succession of crops	14	Control of insects and diseases	33
Rotations	15	Saving surplus vegetables	34
Seed	15	Directions for growing vegetable crops	35

IMPORTANCE OF CITY GARDENS.

A WELL-PLANNED and carefully tended garden is one of the most pleasant and satisfying pieces of work in which the city or suburban family can utilize its spare time. If the soil is properly prepared and a little attention is given the garden as required, the work need not become a burden on the members of the household.

Gardening the back yards and vacant lots of the cities and towns of our country is a worthy endeavor, because it utilizes the spare

FIG. 1.—A group of vegetables harvested at one time from a home garden.

time and labor of persons employed at other work and brings to the family table a greater diversity of food. (Fig. 1.) It also eliminates many undesirable views and eyesores, putting in their places pleasing green growing crops. (Figs. 2 and 3 and title-page illustration.)

Gardening is a patriotic work which will result in both pleasure and profit. It gives pleasure not only in the work with the growing plants, but in the producing of high-quality, crisp, fresh vegetables for the family table. It gives profit by producing vegetables cheaper than they can be purchased and by reducing the need for more expensive foods. (Fig. 4.) Gardening is profitable also because better health is secured by the exercise in the open air and the use of more vegetables in the diet.

Gardening should be an important part of the city and suburban life because of the interest it adds to the lives of people little used to country surroundings. It is interesting to the young and the old, and to women and girls as well as men and boys. There is no better way to keep the boys off the streets and out of mischief than to give them a plat of ground on which they can make a garden (figs. 5 and 6), the results to be their very own. Very young children (fig. 7) can be interested in garden work. One 5-year-old boy in Wash-

FIG. 2.—A city lot which may be used for a garden.

ington, D. C., this past season planted several kinds of seed and grew the plants to maturity. This youngster could be sent to the garden for any one of half a dozen different vegetables and would return with the right one.

TYPES OF GARDENING.

There are several types of gardening which should be of interest in all city and suburban sections. Some of the more important types are back-yard gardens, vacant-lot gardens, and school gardens.

The back-yard garden is probably the most important of the three, because it is more intimately associated with the home. The area

FIG. 3.—A vacant lot the first season after the rubbish had been cleared away and a garden established.

immediately back of the house is the plat usually considered as the back-yard garden. If this spot is not used as a garden it often becomes an unsightly place, and thus gardening improves the home surroundings. (Figs. 8 and 9.)

The condition of the soil in the back yard can be steadily improved year after year as long as the family occupies the house. (Fig. 10.) Its nearness to the house is a great inducement for the family to work the garden and to utilize the crops to the fullest extent.

Vacant-lot gardens are important because of the large areas that can be found for the work.

Commercial truck growers or market gardeners utilize land in the outskirts of cities, but unless this land is very productive or can be had at a low rental for a period of years it will not pay them to lease it. With the use of the home gardener's labor, however, the cropping of these areas can be made remunerative.

Large areas of vacant land may be taken over by a company or organization and divided into a number of small plats which individuals may tend. In some cases large plats have been used as gardens by a number of individuals who shared equally in the labor, expense, and results. This type of community garden is not usually a success unless it can be done by a school or institution which controls all of the work. Figure 11 shows a large area which has been divided into a number of individual gardens, while figure 12 shows a large area used as a garden by a public institution.

School gardens are important because they bring to the child early in life an opportunity to see how plants grow, to identify the kinds of plants that are found in the garden, and to learn some of the economic phases of gardening as applied to the family food supply. (Fig. 13.)

FIG. 4.—A vacant lot after plowing. Four women removed the stones and trash from this plat, planted garden crops, and produced enough vegetables for their families.

Porch and window gardens are not important, but in some of the thickly populated sections of the larger cities this type of gardening is quite often practiced. Window boxes, boxes at the ends of porches or on shed roofs, boxes on the edges of walks or even on the small front lawn, and boxes and barrels on the roofs of tenement and apartment buildings are some of the ways of utilizing small spaces in the growing of plants. In the limited areas of boxes, barrels, etc. (figs. 14 and 15), no large quantity of food can be produced, but the growing of plants can be made an interesting study, besides adding something to the family table. Lettuce, parsley, radishes, onions, and tomatoes are some of the crops best suited for such limited spaces.

Both boys' and girls' clubs and adult clubs may utilize vacant lots or the home back yards. There are a number of kinds of clubs

THE CITY AND SUBURBAN VEGETABLE GARDEN. 7

besides regular garden clubs which have accomplished wonderful results in garden work. (Fig. 16.) Boy-scout troops, girl-scout troops, woodcraft clubs, and other similar organizations are among this class of clubs.

COST AND VALUE OF CROPS FROM HOME GARDENS.

There is a great lack of uniformity in figures collected on the value of garden crops. Prices vary from day to day and also vary in different sections of a city. Some persons figure the value of

FIG. 5.—A lot covered with rubbish. Enthusiasm and labor were required to make this plat into a garden.

their garden products at the highest retail prices; others at wholesale prices. Many children obtain prices for their garden products much greater than market prices.

To give uniformity to the value of garden vegetables, a scale of prices should be established for the city, and all who make records of their gardens should use as a guide the scale set for their city.

The following items of cost and valuation of garden products are offered as suggestions to those interested in gardening campaigns.

Cost of fertilizer, labor, tools, seeds, plants, and spraying material.

(a) Fertilizers: Charge manure at $2.50 per 1½ cubic yards or 2-horse load. This would be equal to two 1-horse loads. Commercial fertilizer and lime should be charged at cost price.

(b) Labor: Include all expense of labor hired.
(c) Tools: Charge at one-fourth the first cost when new.
(d) Seeds: All seeds should be charged at prices at store, whether saved, kept over, or given to you.
(e) Plants: Charge at market prices.
(f) Spraying material: Charge at cost price.

Value of crops.

The value of crops should be figured at the prices given below if of good quality; if not of good quality, reduce the value accordingly. If of extra size and quality or extra early, increase the value.

Beans, Lima (shelled beans), 25 cents per quart.
Beans, snap, 30 cents per peck.
Beets, 50 cents per peck. (50 beets of medium size.)
Cabbages, 5 cents per head.
Cauliflower, 10 cents per head; large, high quality, up to 20 cents.
Carrots, 50 cents per peck. (80 carrots of medium size.)
Celery, 4 cents per stalk.
Sweet corn, 2 cents per ear.
Cucumbers, 2 cents each for large and 50 cents per peck for small pickles.
Eggplants, 5 cents each.
Lettuce, 5 cents per head, or an equal quantity of leaf lettuce.
Muskmelons, 10 cents each.
Onions, 35 cents per peck, dry; 20 cents per quart, for sets; 5 cents a bunch if green.
Parsnips, 40 cents per peck.
Peas, 40 cents per peck.
Peppers, 10 cents per dozen.
Irish potatoes:
    Early, 35 cents per peck.
    Late, 25 cents per peck.
Radishes, 3 cents per bunch.
Salsify, 50 cents per peck.
Spinach, kale, turnip greens, beet greens, mustard, etc., 25 cents per peck.
Squashes:
    Summer, 50 cents per dozen.
    Late, 25 cents each.
Tomatoes:
    Early, 50 cents per peck.
    Main crop, 25 cents per peck.
Turnips, 25 cents per peck.
Watermelons, 25 cents each.

LABOR AND EXPENSE REQUIRED TO MAKE HOME GARDENS.

Persons interested in making a garden often ask how much labor it will take to care properly for a garden of a certain size, and what results should be expected under average conditions.

The following records secured in the District of Columbia are thoroughly reliable and vouched for by the school teachers and leaders who supervised part of the work and by the agricultural agent for the District:

(1) Records from 20 school boys' and girls' home gardens, each of which comprised an area of 500 square feet or more.

> Average area per garden, 1,022 square feet.
> Average expense per garden, $1.38.
> Average hours of labor per garden, 17.

(2) Records from 59 school boys' and girls' home gardens, each of which comprised an area less than 500 square feet.

> Average area per garden, 166 square feet.
> Average expense per garden, 62 cents.
> Average hours of labor per garden, 14.

(3) Records from 8 club boys' and girls' home gardens, each of which comprised an area more than 500 square feet.

> Average area per garden, 1,909 square feet.
> Average expense per garden, $2.51.
> Average hours of labor per garden, 39.

(4) Records from 12 club boys' and girls' home gardens, each of which comprised an area less than 500 square feet.

> Average area per garden, 305 square feet.
> Average expense per garden, 84 cents.
> Average hours of labor per garden, 28.

(5) Records from 50 family home gardens, which comprised areas ranging from 720 to 65,340 square feet.

> Average area per garden, 7,801 square feet.
> Average expense per garden, $13.92.
> Average hours of labor per garden, 132.

From the above records from 149 home gardens, a garden averaging 2,800 square feet will cost $4.82 and will require about 58 hours of labor to take care of it during the season.

The figures in the following table are taken from the records referred to above.

Value of vegetables which a home garden will produce.

Kind of garden.	Number.	Average per garden.				Value per square foot.		Value per acre.	
		Area.	Expense.	Value.	Hours of work.	Gross.	Net.	Gross.	Net.
Boys' and girls' home school gardens:		Sq. ft.							
More than 500 square feet in area..........	20	1,022	$1.38	$7.50	17	$0.00734	$0.006	$319.73	$261.36
Less than 500 square feet in area..........	59	166	.62	2.97	14	.018	.0142	784.08	618.55
Boys' and girls' club gardens:									
More than 500 square feet in area..........	8	1,909	2.51	14.46	39	.0122	.0092	531.43	400.75
Less than 500 square feet in area..........	12	305	.84	6.95	28	.0226	.0197	984.46	858.13
Family home gardens:									
Ranging from 720 to 65,340 square feet....	50	7,801	13.92	70.56	132	.00904	.00726	393.78	316.25
Best garden of large extent...............	1	8,800	25.00	231.82	200	.0263	.0236	1,194.98	1,067.22
Best garden of small extent...............	1	272	.85	9.05	17½	.033	.03	1,437.48	1,306.80

The figures in this table show that the average net value per acre is considerably greater in the gardens of 500 square feet or less than in larger areas. This is shown both in the case of the boys' and girls' home school gardens and in the boys' and girls' home club gardens.

Another convincing point the figures make is that the club gardens produced very much better returns than the home school gardens or the home family gardens. This difference is due, no doubt, to the better supervision given to the club gardens and the greater stimulation due to healthy competition among the members.

LOCATION AND SOIL.

If no yard is available, a suitable vacant lot may be secured. In every case the garden should be near the house, so that it will be possible for the housewife to go into the garden and in a few minutes secure the desired vegetables. When the garden is situated at some distance from the house the effort necessary to care for it becomes a burden, the products are not utilized to the fullest extent, and the garden is soon neglected.

Areas shaded a large portion of the time should not be selected for a garden. (Fig. 17.) The foliage crops, such as lettuce, parsley, and chard, will thrive fairly well when they get three or four hours of sunlight a day. Such crops as tomatoes, eggplants, and peppers

FIG. 6.—The same plat illustrated in figure 5, showing a very profitable vegetable garden maintained by boys assisted by their parents.

THE CITY AND SUBURBAN VEGETABLE GARDEN. 11

FIG. 7.—An example of how children may be interested in garden work. This 3-year-old youngster has spent many hours in the garden and can name many of the matured crops.

should have an abundance of sunshine, at least five or six hours each day. (Fig. 18.)

Most city gardeners are handicapped in that they must make the best of the space and soil available to them. While a sandy loam with a well-drained southern exposure will give better results than less favored locations, the gardener should not be deterred from making an effort even though his location is not the best.

Almost any kind of soil, unless it is composed of bricks, mortar, stone, rubbish, etc., can be used for gardening if it is properly handled. Heavy clay soils may be improved greatly by adding large quantities of strawy manure in the fall or by turning under green-manure crops. It is usually practicable to cover the clay soil with 2 or 3 inches of sifted coal ashes and then thoroughly incorporate the two by spading and hoeing. Sandy soils may be decidedly improved for gardening purposes by growing green-manure crops on the land or by turning under liberal quantities of stable manure.

Good drainage is very important in the garden, and if the soil is not naturally well drained it should be drained artificially. Tile drains are most satisfactory for the garden, but open ditches may be used.

SIZE OF THE GARDEN.

The city back yard is seldom large enough to produce sufficient vegetables for the average family. On limited areas of 800 square feet or less, only such crops as lettuce, snap beans, onions, radishes, a few tomato plants, spinach, kale, chard, beets, and other crops requiring little space should be grown. (Fig. 19.) Where more space is available, a quarter acre may be profitably employed, and where sweet corn and sweet and Irish potatoes are to be grown a half acre is none too much. (Fig. 20.) The keynote to success in the garden is to have the soil as fertile as possible, so as to produce sufficient vegetables with the least amount of labor.

Fig. 8.—A back yard after being cleaned up and planted to early Irish potatoes.

A small garden well cared for is far better than a larger garden which is neglected.

ARRANGEMENT OF THE GARDEN.

The arrangement of the garden should be carefully worked out to suit the conditions of each particular garden. In the winter, when there is usually plenty of time available, it is a good plan to sit down with paper, pencil, and rule and draw up a plan of the garden. Mark on this plan the location for each vegetable and the area covered, the successions, date of planting, etc. By making a plan and following it throughout the season the greatest success will be had with the garden.

While each garden must be planned to suit the conditions, there are a few general rules which apply to all gardens. The rows should run north and south, to give the best distribution of sunlight on all sides of the plants, but where it is more convenient, and where washing must be prevented, the rows can run in other directions. All permanent vegetables, such as rhubarb, asparagus, and herbs, should be planted at one side of the garden, where they will not be disturbed every year. Tall vegetables, like corn and pole beans, should be put in a position where they will not shade the small vegetables. Wherever the land is available and horse cultivation can be used, allow

FIG. 9.—The same area shown in figure 8 later in the season. Beans, chard, and cabbages have followed the potatoes, and Lima beans have covered the board fence.

sufficient space between rows for the larger cultivating tools. Also run the rows the long way of the garden in order to avoid excessive turning at the ends of the rows. (Fig. 21.) For horse cultivation provide a 4 or 5 foot pathway along two sides of the garden at right angles to the rows, so that turning with the cultivator can be managed without injuring the vegetables. All vegetables that are to be planted early and that require early cultivation should be grouped at one side of the garden, to facilitate cultivation. Figure 22 may offer many suggestions as to the arrangement and location of the crops in a quarter-acre garden. The distances given for rows are for horse cultivation.

FENCES AND WINDBREAKS.

Every garden should be surrounded by a fence to keep out stray dogs, cats, chickens, and small children. In the prairie regions a windbreak or shelter belt is absolutely necessary to protect the garden, and in other regions, while not so necessary, a windbreak may protect the crops from damage by strong winds, and the protection from cold winds may lengthen the crop-growing season considerably. If buildings, a grove of trees, a row of evergreens, or a hedge are not available as a windbreak, a tight board fence may be erected, which will serve the double purpose of a fence and a windbreak.

SUCCESSION OF CROPS.

To make a garden yield the maximum quantity of vegetables it is necessary that the land be occupied as much of the time as possible. In some sections three or more crops may be grown on the same land during the season. (Fig. 23.) Care must be used in selecting the crops that are to follow the early-season crops. The vegetable used for the first planting, or one with the same characters or belonging to the same family, should not be used in the same place at the second planting. Cabbage, kale, mustard, Brussels sprouts, and

FIG. 10.—A portion of a prize-winning garden in Washington, D. C. This garden soil has been improved every year for a period of five years. The value of the crop in 1917 was at the rate of $1,149.98 per acre on an area of 8,800 square feet.

FIG. 11.—A portion of a large field which has been divided into a number of individual gardens. Each garden is 25 by 40 feet. The plat in the foreground was planted entirely to tomatoes. Many such fields may be plowed and put under cultivation as vegetable gardens.

cauliflower should not follow each other, for the same insects and diseases affect all these plants; and for the same reason peppers, eggplants, and tomatoes should not follow each other. In many cases, especially in the more southern sections of the country, after an early vegetable is harvested, if no other vegetable is to be planted until autumn, the ground may be planted with cowpeas or some other leguminous crop which can be turned under in preparing for the fall crop.

ROTATIONS.

The rotation of crops is very important in the garden, both in conserving plant food and in checking the spread of insects and diseases. Space which has been occupied by a diseased crop should not be replanted the following year with the same or a closely related crop. It is a good plan to rotate the entire garden every year with an equal-sized plat which has been planted to clover or cowpeas. (Fig. 24.) If such an extra plat is not available, the locations of the various vegetables may be changed each succeeding year. Following root crops, such as parsnips, beets, and carrots, with foliage crops, like kale, cabbage, collards, and lettuce, or with crops like tomatoes, beans, melons, or peppers, will tend to conserve the plant food in the soil and prevent heavy infestations of insects and plant diseases.

SEED.

As soon as the location for the garden is selected and a plan made showing the kinds of vegetables to be grown and the places for planting them, the question of varieties should be decided. A number of points should be considered in selecting the varieties to grow, among them being the time of maturity, the adaptation of the variety to the local conditions, and the quality of the vegetable produced. Usually it is better to select only standard varieties that do well in the locality, but a few novelties may be tried in a small way. With the exception of tomatoes and corn it is often better to select a few varieties and plant these in succession than to procure a larger number of early and late varieties.

Vegetable seed should be purchased several weeks ahead of the time it is to be used, and it is advisable to procure the seed only from reliable seedsmen. A good plan is to procure several descriptive catalogues either from reliable local seedsmen or from other

Fig. 12.—An area devoted to vegetables at an industrial school for girls.

good seed houses. These catalogues should be secured in the winter, so that the selection of seed may be made at leisure moments and the order sent out early.

The quantity of seed to purchase will depend upon the preferences for different vegetables and the size of the garden. The table on page 28 gives the amount of seed necessary for a 50-foot row of the various garden crops.

Buy only first-class seed, for inferior seed will be expensive at any price. Buy only the quantity of seed actually needed for your garden. To buy more may deprive another of a garden.

Seed which has been left from the preceding season should be tested by counting out 25 to 50 seeds of each variety, putting them in a plate between two sheets of moist cloth or blotting paper, and covering with another plate. By looking at the seed every day, the promptness and percentage of germination can be ascertained. Good grades of most garden seeds should germinate 60 to 85 per cent in five or six days. Seeds that send out strong sprouts in a few days have the vitality necessary to insure a good stand of plants, and this is an important item in garden work.

PLANTS.

Plants for the garden can be grown in a limited way in shallow boxes or flats set in a sunny window of the dwelling house. (Fig.

FIG. 13.—A city lot made into a school garden. The children work the garden under the supervision of the teacher. This garden during the season of 1917 produced vegetables to the value of $125.

25.) The soil for the seed boxes should be fine and mellow, and the seed should be planted in rows, with a label to designate each variety or kind. As soon as the plants form three or four leaves they should be transplanted into other boxes, the plants being set at least 2 inches apart each way. Where there is not sufficient space in the house for growing all the plants desired, it is possible to grow the seedlings inside and transplant them into a coldframe out of doors.

All seedlings grown in boxes or flats should be transplanted at least once before they are ready to set in the garden. This transplanting causes the plant to become stocky and to produce a mass of fine roots. (Fig. 26.) In many cases the seedlings are transplanted from the seed flats into earthen pots or dirt bands. Plants from the pots or bands can be set in the garden without disturbing the roots, and the plants receive no check in their growth. By this means it is possible to have plants ready to set in the garden at any time when another crop is taken out. For example, as fast as early cabbages are cut, tomato plants can be set in their places, and pepper plants may be set in the row as fast as the early lettuce is harvested, etc.

HOTBEDS AND COLDFRAMES.

A hotbed and a coldframe of some form are very necessary to secure the maximum benefits from the garden. Plants can be

Fig. 14.—Barrels utilized for growing vegetables. These were filled two-thirds full of ashes, and a foot of soil on top was supplied by a gardener who had time and energy to devote to a very limited area in a congested section of Washington, D. C.

raised more satisfactorily and on a much larger scale with frames than with seed boxes set in the house window. The frames can also be used for maturing early crops and for carrying over crops into the winter.

A very serviceable frame for a hotbed or coldframe may be constructed like the one shown in figure 27. Oak or cypress boards 1 inch thick may be used. A more permanent frame can be constructed by using concrete. A hotbed 6 by 6 feet will be sufficient for the needs of most home gardens, and a coldframe of equal size will be found of great assistance in growing crops successfully.

MAKING A HOTBED.

To make a hotbed, secure a quantity of fresh horse manure, consisting of about two parts of the solid excrement to one part of litter. Pile in a heap under cover for a few days, so that it will heat, and turn it over a few times to mix it thoroughly. When mixed, place the manure in a pile to a depth of 18 inches, keeping it well trampled while being placed. On top of this manure place the frame and pack manure tightly all around it. Place inside the frame 3 to 4 inches of rich soil and cover with a glass sash. Window sash can often be used for this purpose. The bed should stand for several days, some ventilation being given meanwhile,

FIG. 15.—The other side of the yard seen in figure 14. For several months this garden supplied two elderly people with fresh vegetables.

so that the gases from the manure may escape. When the temperature of the bed has fallen to between 80° and 90° F., the seed may be planted.

Another very satisfactory method of constructing a hotbed is to dig a pit to a depth of 18 to 24 inches and in this pack the manure and place the frame over it. This method has the advantage of requiring less manure. In using either method it is a good plan in the fall to cover the ground where the hotbed is to be located with a layer of manure about a foot thick. This covering will keep the soil soft and warm, which will be a great aid when the time comes to construct the hotbed

Fig. 16.—A 10-year-old boy in his club garden containing 272 square feet. The result of his labor was $9.05 worth of vegetables.

A hotbed may often be constructed adjoining the house and a pipe from the house heating system used to furnish heat for the bed.

MANAGEMENT OF A HOTBED.

When the temperature of a hotbed has fallen to the required degree, the soil is raked until very fine and all strawy material and refuse removed. The seed is planted in rows 3 inches apart and to a depth of an eighth to a half inch, according to the size of the seed. A thin stick or a lath can be pressed into the soil to give the required depth and to mark the rows. The seed should be covered very lightly with soil.

As the plants grow, they should be watered often enough to keep the soil from drying out, but not enough to keep the soil water-soaked. Water should be applied in a fine spray, and this can be done by using a fine sprinkler on the hose or watering can. The watering should be done early in the day, so that the plants will have time to dry off before night.

Plants should have plenty of fresh air, but should not receive a direct draft or air that is chilly enough to check their growth. The hotbed sash may be raised slightly in the morning after the air becomes warm, but it should be lowered again before it turns cold toward evening. The sash should be opened only on the side opposite from the direction of the wind. On a bright sunny day the sash may be raised several inches, but on a dull day only a very small opening should be made. Always give good ventilation after watering the plants. When the plants become large and the weather is warm, the sash is left off gradually for longer periods, in order to harden the plants.

Such plants as are being grown for setting in the garden should be transplanted into the coldframe as soon as they are about 2 inches high and have three or four leaves. Plants which are to mature crops in the hotbed should be thinned out as soon as they begin to crowd in the row. The soil should be stirred several times and all weeds taken out as soon as they appear. A hand weeder is a useful tool for this purpose.

Radish, lettuce, onions, etc., can be produced very early in the spring in the hotbed. Tomato, cabbage, celery, cauliflower, eggplant, pepper, and kohl-rabi plants should be started in the hotbed in order to have them ready for planting in early spring.

USE OF COLDFRAMES.

A coldframe usually is only a sash-covered frame placed over a portion of good garden soil. No heat is supplied except what comes from the sun. A coldframe is used to protect tender plants during the early spring or late autumn. The management of a coldframe is very similar to that of a hotbed both in regard to watering and in ventilating.

FIG. 17.—An area completely shaded for more than three or four hours of the day. Such areas should never be planted.

FERTILIZING THE GARDEN.

The soil used for growing vegetables should be very rich and well supplied with humus. To produce vegetables of high quality and in a short period of time it is necessary to have large amounts of readily available plant food. Well-rotted stable manure is probably the best fertilizer, because it supplies both the plant food and humus. Wherever it is possible to obtain sufficient manure it should be applied at the rate of 1 to 2 pounds per square foot or a good wheelbarrow load or two to each square rod, depending on the character of the soil. If sufficient manure is not obtainable it can be supplemented by using commercial fertilizer. An application of 3 to 6 pounds per

FIG. 18.—An area which receives more than five hours' sunlight in a day. Such areas can be made into successful gardens.

square rod of a high-grade mixture analyzing 8 to 10 per cent phosphoric acid, 2 to 4 per cent nitrogen, and 1 to 3 per cent potash will be satisfactory on many garden soils.

Prepared sheep manure is an excellent fertilizer if it can be obtained at a reasonable price. Nitrate of soda is often used to hasten the growth of some plants. The best method of using nitrate of soda is to dissolve a teaspoonful in a gallon of water and use the solution to water the plants. Do not sprinkle nitrate of soda water over the leaves of the plants, for concentrated solutions are likely to burn the leaves.

When coarse or strawy manure is used it should be applied and plowed under in the fall, but if the stable manure is well rotted it may be applied as a top-dressing and plowed under in the spring. Commercial fertilizer may be applied broadcast over the land after spading and thoroughly mixed with the soil by hoeing and raking, or it may be applied under the row.

A compost heap will furnish plant food that is in a quickly available condition and also soil which can be used in the hotbed, coldframe, and seed flats, and to put under and around plants which require considerable quantities of nitrogen. Such plants as cucumbers, cantaloupes, watermelons, and squashes will be greatly benefited if good compost is used in the hill when the seed is planted.

A compost heap can be easily made. First, select a place near the garden, but screened from view. Put down a layer of sods and over

FIG. 19.—A limited space which may be planted to crops such as tomatoes, cabbage, lettuce, snap beans, beets, kale, and radish, with Lima beans on the fence.

this place alternate layers of manure, sandy soil, and clay soil until the pile is of the desired height. The whole compost pile should be cut down and turned several times during the season, and by the next spring the manure will be thoroughly decayed and mixed with the soil. In the more thickly populated sections of a city compost heaps are not usually allowed, so compost or decayed manure will have to be hauled in from out of the city.

It is often possible for the manure from city stables to be collected, taken to dumps located in the suburbs, and there composted. From this source city gardeners may be supplied.

FIG. 20.—A large area which may be planted to crops that require plenty of room. This garden is planted to sweet corn, peas, sweet potatoes, peppers, etc.

The supply of commercial fertilizer should be conserved to the utmost. A satisfactory fertilizer may be had by using 40 pounds of chicken or pigeon manure, both of which are especially rich in nitrogen, 5 to 8 pounds of unleached hardwood ashes, and 5 to 8 pounds of acid phosphate per square rod. The chicken or pigeon manure should be applied separately, as a loss of nitrogen will result if it is mixed with the other ingredients. Many homes burn sufficient wood to produce the necessary quantity of ashes, and comparatively little care is required to collect and save them, while chicken manure is available to most gardeners. Acid phosphate is relatively cheap and comparatively plentiful, but if so desired bone meal may be substituted for it.

LIMING.

Lime added to the soil will help to break up the soil particles and will also correct any acid or sour condition. Lime is not a plant food, but it aids in making the plant food in the soil more available.

Lime may be applied to the soil in the form of burned lime, hydrated lime, or finely ground limestone. Finely ground limestone may be applied either in the fall or in the spring. Burned lime or hydrated lime should not be applied in connection with stable manure because it liberates a great deal of the ammonia in the manure. The manure may be spread on the land and spaded or plowed under. The lime may be scattered over the spaded soil and worked in by hoeing and raking, or by harrowing. If the manure is applied in the fall the lime may be applied in the spring.

From 5 to 8 pounds per square rod of burned lime or hydrated lime will be a sufficient application and may be repeated every three or four years.

Although a garden soil may be tested with litmus paper to see if it is in need of lime, a good plan for most gardeners is to use lime anyway. Lime is comparatively cheap, and for the limited areas of most city gardens the expense will be small.

PREPARING THE SOIL.

The garden soil should be thoroughly prepared. A deep seed bed (8 to 10 inches) with the soil loose and mellow to the full depth is very essential. Heavy lands should be plowed or spaded in the fall

FIG. 21.—Long straight rows of vegetables which add attractiveness to a garden and lessen the labor of cultivation. Note how this garden has produced these results.

if there is no danger of washing and replowed or dug up with a mattock in the spring. Land that it is not advisable to plow in the fall should be plowed as early in the spring as possible. If there is plenty of humus in the soil or some green-manure crop is turned under, the soil will crumble and a fine seed bed can be easily prepared. If the soil is heavy and is lacking in humus it is inclined to stick together and bake, and it is a difficult matter to pulverize it sufficiently for gardening work. Care must be used to cover all sod and strawy material, so they will quickly decay and not interfere with garden operations.

Often the ground of back yards or vacant lots selected for gardens has been hardened by much trampling, and the soil can not be put

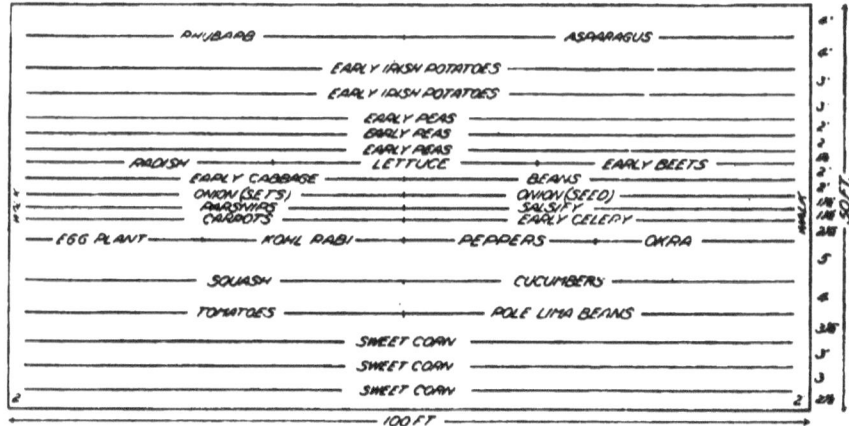

Fig. 22.—Diagram showing the location and arrangement of crops in a garden about a quarter of an acre in area.

into proper condition without the expenditure of considerable labor. The task of digging up such soil for the first time is very arduous, but it does not pay to slight the work. Spading to a depth of 8 inches and loosening 2 inches below the spade depth is very essential. Fining the soil all the way is also necessary.

TOOLS.

A spade or spading fork, a hoe, a rake, a dibble or trowel, and a line are the essential tools required for a small garden. There are a few more tools, however, which are very desirable for certain kinds of work. Some of these tools are a mattock, a garden hose or a watering can, a wheelbarrow, a shovel, a hand weeder of some form, and a hand wheel cultivator. Some of the tools mentioned are shown in figures 28, 29, and 30.

LAYING OFF.

It is a simple matter to take the plan which has been made of the garden and lay off the distance on the opposite sides of the garden and set a stake at each place. By stretching a line between the stakes it is possible to secure straight rows, which add attractiveness to the garden. Straight, long rows are usually the first points to be noticed by any judge of a garden.

SEEDING.

In a small vegetable garden the seed is sown by hand, and with such crops as lettuce, radishes, onions, and beets is sown thicker

FIG. 23.—An illustration of companion plantings and succession of crops. Radishes are shown planted between onions and sweet corn (not yet up) between snap beans. All the area was later planted to navy beans.

than the plants need to be, so as to insure a stand. Later, the extra plants are removed, leaving only the strongest and best. Extreme care should be taken to use no more seed than absolutely necessary. The usual tendency is to sow too thickly. All small seed is sown to a depth of a quarter to three-quarters of an inch, depending upon the soil and the season, while larger seeds, like corn, beans, and peas, are sown to a depth of 2 inches.

A CITY GARDENER'S PLANTING TABLE.

Distances apart for rows and plants, depths of planting, quantity of seeds and number of plants required for 50 feet of row, and time required for growth.

Kind of vegetable.	Distance apart.		Depth for planting seed.	Seed and plants for 50 feet of row.		Time until ready for use (days).
	Rows.	Plants in the row.		Seed.	Plants.	
			Inches.			
Asparagus	2 feet	15 inches	1 to 1½	½ ounce	30 to 40	
Bean:						
Bush	do	3 to 4 inches	1½ to 2	½ pint		40 to 65
Bush Lima	2½ feet	6 to 10 inches	1½ to 2	¼ to ½ pint		70 to 90
Pole Lima	3 feet	3 to 4 feet	1½ to 2	¼ pint		80 to 120
Beet	15 to 18 inches	4 to 5 inches	1 to 1½	1 ounce		60 to 80
Cabbage	2 to 2½ feet	15 to 20 inches	½	¼ ounce	30 to 45	90 to 130
Carrot	15 to 18 inches	3 to 4 inches	½	½ ounce		70 to 100
Cauliflower	2 to 2½ feet	15 to 18 inches	½	1/16 ounce	30 to 40	100 to 130
Celery	18 to 24 inches	4 to 6 inches	½	do	100 to 125	120 to 150
Collard	do	12 to 18 inches	½	¼ ounce	30 to 50	100 to 120
Corn, sweet	2½ to 3 feet	10 to 12 inches	2	¼ pint		60 to 100
Cucumber	4 to 5 feet	15 inches	1 to 1½	¼ ounce		60 to 80
Eggplant	2 to 2½ feet	18 to 24 inches	½	¼ ounce	25 to 35	100 to 140
Kale	18 to 24 inches	8 to 10 inches	½	¼ ounce		90 to 120
Lettuce	15 to 18 inches	6 to 10 inches	½	do	60 to 100	60 to 90
Melons:						
Muskmelon	5 to 6 feet	Drills 18 inches; Hills 5 feet	1 to 1½	do		120 to 150
Watermelon	8 to 10 feet	Drills 2 to 3 feet; Hills 8 feet	1 to 2	½ ounce		100 to 120
Okra	3 feet	2 feet	1 to 2	1 ounce		90 to 140
Onion:						
Seed	15 inches	3 to 4 inches	½ to 1	½ ounce		130 to 150
Sets	do	do	1 to 2	½ quart		60 to 120
Parsley	do	do	½	¼ ounce		90 to 120
Parsnip	15 to 18 inches	do	½ to 1	¼ ounce		125 to 160
Pea	2½ to 3 feet	1 inch	2 to 3	½ to 1 pint		40 to 80
Potatoes:						
Irish	2 to 2½ feet	12 to 18 inches	4	2 to 3 lbs.		80 to 140
Sweet	4 to 5 feet	14 to 18 inches	2 to 3	2 pounds	([1])	140 to 160
Radish	12 to 15 inches	1 inch	½ to 1	½ ounce		20 to 140
Salsify	15 to 18 inches	1 to 2 inches	½ to 1	do		120 to 180
Spinach	do	do	1 to 2	do		30 to 60
Squash:						
Bush	3 to 4 feet	Drills 15 to 18 inches; Hills 4 feet	1 to 2	¼ ounce		60 to 80
Vine	7 to 10 feet	Drills 2 to 3 feet; Hills 8 feet	1 to 2	do		120 to 160
Tomato	2 to 3 feet	2 to 3 feet	½ to 1	1/16 ounce	15 to 25	80 to 125
Turnip	15 to 18 inches	2 to 3 inches	¼ to ½	¼ ounce		60 to 80

[1] 50 slips.

TIME OF PLANTING.

Garden crops may be divided into four groups, as follows:

Group 1.—Those vegetables that may be planted some two weeks before the last killing frost. These include cabbage plants, radish, collards, onions (sets), early smooth peas, kale, lettuce (seed in boxes), early potatoes, turnips, and mustard.

Group 2.—Those that may be planted about the date of the last killing frost. These include beets, parsnips, carrots, lettuce, salsify, spinach, wrinkled peas, cauliflower, celery, onions (seed), parsley, lettuce (in open ground), chard, and Chinese cabbage.

Group 3.—Those plants that can not be planted until all danger of frost is past. These include snap beans, sweet corn, okra, and tomatoes (plants).

THE CITY AND SUBURBAN VEGETABLE GARDEN.   29

Group 4.—Heat-loving plants that can not be safely planted until the ground is warm, such as Lima beans, peppers (plants), eggplant, cucumbers, melons, squash, and sweet potatoes. The table gives the dates in the different zones for all garden crops.

Most gardeners are interested in knowing the earliest dates for planting the various crops, as earliness is much desired. It has been found that the earliest safe dates for planting garden crops can be determined from the average dates of the last killing frost in spring.

FIG. 24.—Cowpeas planted as a rotation crop, to be turned under in order to improve the soil.

The map (fig. 31) divides the continental portion of the United States into zones, with a difference between them of about two weeks in the average date of the last killing frost. The average dates of the last killing frost, while a guide in planting, can not be depended upon every year, but are reasonably safe. There is a difference of several days within the zones themselves, owing to difference in elevation, in latitude, and in proximity to bodies of water. The following table gives the earliest safe dates for planting the various vegetables in the open in the different zones illustrated in figure 31.

EARLIEST PLANTING DATES.

Earliest safe dates for planting vegetables in the open in the zones shown in figure 31.

Crop.	Zone A.	Zone B.	Zone C.	Zone D.	Zone E.	Zone F.	Zone G.
Asparagus	(Not grown)	Feb. 15 to Mar. 1	Mar. 1 to 15	Mar. 15 to Apr. 15	Apr. 15 to May 1	May 1 to 15	May 1 to June 1.
Artichoke {Globe	Mar. 1 to 15	Mar. 15 to Apr. 1	Apr. 1 to 15	Apr. 15 to May 15	May 1 to 30	(Not grown)	(Not grown).
{Jerusalem	Feb. 1 to 15	Feb. 15 to Mar. 1	Mar. 1 to 15	Mar. 15 to Apr. 1	Apr. 1 to 15	May 1 to 30	Do.
Bean {Lima	Mar. 1 to Apr. 1	Mar. 1 to Apr. 1	Apr. 1 to 15	May 1 to 15	May 15 to June 1	May 15 to June 15	May 15 to June 15.
{Snap	Feb. 15 to Mar. 1	Mar. 1 to 15	Mar. 15 to 30	Apr. 1 to May 1	May 1 to 15	May 15 to June 1	May 15 to June 1.
Beet	Feb. 1 to 15	Feb. 15 to Mar. 1	Mar. 1 to 15	Mar. 15 to Apr. 15	Apr. 15 to May 1	May 1 to 15	May 15 to June 1.
Brussels sprouts	do	do	do	do	do	do	Do.
Cabbage	Jan. 1 to Feb. 1	Jan. 15 to Feb. 15	Feb. 15 to Mar. 1	Mar. 1 to 15	Mar. 15 to Apr. 15	Apr. 15 to May 1	May 1 to May 15.
Carrot	Feb. 1 to 15	Feb. 15 to Mar. 1	Mar. 1 to 15	Mar. 15 to Apr. 15	Apr. 15 to May 1	May 1 to 15	May 1 to June 1.
Cauliflower	do	do	do	do	do	do	Do.
Celery	do	do	do	do	do	do	Do.
Chard	do	do	do	do	do	do	Do.
Collard	Jan. 1 to Feb. 1	Feb. 1 to 15	Feb. 15 to Mar. 1	Mar. 1 to 15	Mar. 15 to Apr. 15	May 1 to June 1	May 15 to June 15.
Corn, sweet	Feb. 15 to Mar. 1	Mar. 1 to 15	Mar. 15 to Apr. 1	Apr. 1 to May 1	Apr. 15 to May 15	May 15 to June 15	June 1 to 15.
Cucumber	Mar. 1 to 15	Mar. 15 to Apr. 1	Apr. 1 to 15	Apr. 15 to May 1	May 1 to June 1	do	do
Eggplant	do	do	do	do	do	do	May 1 to 15.
Garlic	Jan. 1 to Feb. 1	Feb. 1 to 15	Feb. 15 to Mar. 1	Mar. 1 to 15	Mar. 15 to Apr. 15	Apr. 15 to May 1	do
Kale	do	do	do	do	do	do	Do.
Kohl-rabi	Feb. 1 to 15	Feb. 15 to Mar. 1	Mar. 1 to 15	Mar. 15 to Apr. 15	Apr. 1 to May 1	May 1 to 15	May 15 to June 1.
Lettuce {Head	do	do	do	do	do	do	Do.
{Leaf	Jan. 1 to Feb. 1	Feb. 1 to 15	Feb. 15 to Mar. 1	Mar. 1 to 15	Mar. 15 to Apr. 15	Apr. 15 to May 1	May 1 to May 15.
Melons	Mar. 1 to 15	Mar. 15 to Apr. 1	Apr. 1 to 15	Apr. 15 to May 1	May 1 to June 1	June 1 to 15	May 15 to June 1.
Mustard	Feb. 1 to 15	Feb. 15 to Mar. 1	Mar. 1 to 15	Mar. 15 to Apr. 1	Apr. 1 to May 1	May 15 to June 1	June 1 to 15.
Okra, or gumbo	Feb. 15 to Mar. 1	Mar. 1 to Mar. 15	Mar. 15 to 30	Apr. 1 to May 1	May 1 to 15	May 1 to 15	May 1 to 15.
Onion {Seed	Feb. 1 to 15	Feb. 15 to Mar. 1	Mar. 1 to 15	Mar. 15 to Apr. 1	Apr. 1 to May 1	Apr. 15 to May 1	May 15 to June 1.
{Sets	Jan. 1 to Feb. 1	Feb. 1 to 15	Feb. 15 to Mar. 1	Mar. 1 to 15	Mar. 15 to Apr. 15	May 1 to 15	May 1 to June 1.
Parsley	Feb. 1 to 15	Feb. 15 to Mar. 1	Mar. 1 to 15	Mar. 15 to Apr. 15	Apr. 15 to May 15	May 1 to 15	May 15 to June 1.
Parsnip	do	do	do	do	do	do	Do.
Peas {Smooth	Jan. 1 to Feb. 1	Feb. 1 to 15	Feb. 15 to Mar. 1	Mar. 1 to 15	Mar. 15 to Apr. 15	Apr. 15 to May 1	May 1 to June 1.
{Wrinkled	Feb. 1 to 15	Feb. 15 to Mar. 1	Mar. 1 to 15	Mar. 15 to Apr. 15	Apr. 1 to May 1	May 1 to 15	May 15 to June 1.
Peppers	Mar. 1 to 15	Mar. 15 to Apr. 1	Apr. 1 to 15	Apr. 15 to May 1	May 1 to June 1	June 1 to 15	do
Potatoes {Irish	Jan. 1 to Feb. 1	Feb. 1 to 15	Feb. 15 to Mar. 1	Mar. 1 to 15	Mar. 15 to Apr. 15	Apr. 15 to May 1	May 1 to June 1.
{Sweet	Mar. 1 to 15	Mar. 15 to Apr. 1	Apr. 1 to May 1	Apr. 15 to May 1	May 1 to June 1	June 1 to 15	May 1 to June 1.
Pumpkin	do	do	do	do	do	do	Do.
Radish	Jan. 1 to Feb. 1	Feb. 1 to 15	Feb. 15 to Mar. 1	Mar. 1 to 15	Mar. 15 to Apr. 15	Apr. 15 to May 1	May 1 to 15.
Rhubarb	(Not grown)	(Not grown)	do	Mar. 15 to Apr. 15	Apr. 15 to May 1	May 1 to 15	May 15 to June 1.
Salsify	Feb. 1 to 15	Feb. 15 to Mar. 1	Mar. 1 to 15	Mar. 1 to 15	May 1 to June 1	May 1 to June 1	Do.
Spinach	do	do	do	do	do	do	Do.
Squash	Mar. 1 to 15	Mar. 15 to Apr. 1	Apr. 1 to 15	Apr. 15 to May 1	May 1 to June 1	June 1 to 15	June 1 to 15.
Tomato	do	do	do	do	do	May 1 to June 15	
Turnip	Jan. 1 to Feb. 1	Feb. 1 to 15	Feb. 15 to Mar. 1	Mar. 1 to 15	Mar. 15 to Apr. 15	Apr. 15 to May 1	May 1 to May 15.

LATEST PLANTING DATES.

Latest safe dates for planting vegetables for the fall garden in the zones[1] shown in figure 32.

Crop.	Zone C.	Zone D.	Zone E.	Zone F.	Zone G.
Bean:					
Bush	Sept. 15	Sept. 1	Aug. 15	Aug. 1	July 15
Pole Lima	...do....	Aug. 1	July 15	July 1	
Beet	...do....	Sept. 1	Aug. 15	Aug. 1	July 15
Cabbage	Sept. 1	Aug. 15	July 15	July 1	June 15
Carrot	...do....	...do....	...do....	...do....	Do.
Cauliflower	...do....	...do....	...do....	...do....	Do.
Celery	Oct. 1	Sept. 1	Aug. 1	...do....	May 15
Chard, Swiss	Sept. 15	...do....	Aug. 15	Aug. 1	July 15
Corn, sweet	Aug. 15	Aug. 1	July 15	July 1	June 15
Cucumber	...do....	...do....	...do....	...do....	
Eggplant	July 15	July 1	June 15	June 1	
Kale	Nov. 1	Oct. 1	Sept. 15	Sept. 1	Aug. 15
Lettuce	...do....	Oct. 15	Oct. 1	Sept. 15	Sept. 1
Melons:					
Muskmelon	June 15	June 1	May 15	May 1	
Watermelon	July 1	July 1	June 15		
Okra	July 15	...do....	...do....	June 1	
Onion:					
Seed	June 15	June 1	May 15	May 1	Apr. 15
Sets	July 15	July 1	June 15	June 1	May 15
Parsley	Nov. 1	Oct. 1	Sept. 1	Aug. 1	July 1
Parsnip			May 15	May 1	Apr. 15
Pea	Nov. 1	Oct. 1	Sept. 1	Aug. 1	July 15
Peppers	July 15	July 1	June 15	June 1	
Potatoes:					
Irish	Aug. 15	Aug. 1	July 15	July 1	June 15
Sweet	...do....	July 15	June 15	May 1	
Radish	Oct. 15	Oct. 1	Sept. 15	Sept. 1	Aug. 15
Salsify	June 15	June 1	May 15	May 1	Apr. 15
Spinach	Oct. 15	Oct. 1	Sept. 1	Aug. 15	Aug. 1
Squash:					
Bush	Aug. 15	Aug. 1	July 15	July 1	June 15
Vine	July 15	July 1	June 15	June 1	
Tomato	Aug. 15	July 15	July 1	June 15	
Turnip	Oct. 15	Oct. 1	Sept. 1	Aug. 1	July 15

[1] Zones A and B are sections in which many vegetables are planted late in the fall to form the winter garden or early spring garden.

Many crops may be used to make a fall garden, and the latest safe dates for planting in the various zones are shown in the above table, which is to be used in connection with the zones shown in figure 32.

SETTING PLANTS.

The soil where plants are to be set should be worked up fine to a depth of several inches, in order to facilitate planting. The plants should be

FIG. 25.—A flat, or seed box, useful for starting plants to be planted very early in the season.

thoroughly watered an hour or so before removing them from the flats or frames, to insure the adherence of the earth to the roots. If the plants have not been transplanted into pots or dirt bands, they should be removed with a ball of earth attached to the roots.

A cloudy day or just before nightfall is the best time to set out plants, though potted plants and plants in dirt bands may be set at any time with good results. The plants should be set a trifle deeper than they were in the seed bed and the soil firmed around each plant from the bottom of the hole to the surface. A trowel or a dibble can be used for making the holes to receive the plants. If water is to be used in setting the plants, it should be poured about the plant when the hole is partially filled with soil. The moist earth is then covered with dry soil, which prevents the rapid evaporation of the moisture.

Cabbage and lettuce plants may be set in the open as soon as the ground can be worked in the spring, but many plants, such as the tomato, pepper, and eggplant, should not be set out until the weather has become warm, as indicated in the table and the zone maps. Some time may be gained by setting the tender plants before danger of frost is over and then protecting them by covering with newspapers, tin cans, berry boxes, or plant covers. These covers may be put over the plants at night when frosts are likely to occur, and if partially removed in the morning they will shade the newly set plants.

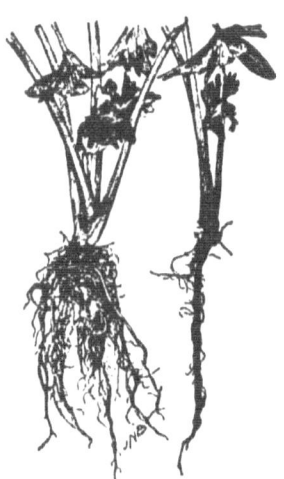

Fig. 25.—Celery plants, showing the effect of transplanting on the root system.

CULTIVATION.

Thorough preparation of the seed bed and good seed properly planted are very essential for successful gardens, but unless the plants are properly cultivated during the season the garden will prove a failure. Cultivation is not entirely for the purpose of killing the weeds, but has as its main object the conserving of soil moisture. Frequent shallow cultivation forms a soil mulch which prevents the loss of moisture, and frequent stirring prevents the growth of weeds. The soil close to the plants should be kept fine and free from weeds, the same as the spaces between the rows. If the cultivation is begun as soon as the plants show and is kept up at regular intervals throughout the season, the work does not become burdensome. If cultivation is given only occasionally, the plants may suffer (fig. 33), and the work is arduous and unsatisfactory. Cultivate the land after every rain, so as to break up the crust that has formed, and give other cultivation as needed to form a soil mulch and keep down weeds.

If the garden has been laid out with long rows and a medium-wide space between the rows, most of the cultivation may be done with a hand cultivator. With such a cultivator the work may be very quickly and efficiently done. In many instances very efficient work can be done with a hoe, but the larger share of the work of cultivating can be performed much more quickly with a hand cultivator.

IRRIGATION.

A good supply of water in the soil is necessary throughout the growing season, to enable the plants to grow vigorously. Many times during long periods of hot, dry weather the supply of moisture in the soil becomes very low, and the plants are so checked in growth that they fail to produce any crop, or at best produce a very poor one. Where a supply of water is available it is often possible to establish

FIG. 27.—A suitable frame for carrying sash for a coldframe or hotbed for a city garden.

an irrigation system which will insure an abundance of water for the plants at a relatively small expense.

Several systems of irrigation are adapted to the garden. An overhead system is probably best. By one such system the water is applied by means of elevated pipes placed at regular intervals over the garden. Nozzles are set in these pipes every 2 feet, and the pressure on the water forces out a fine stream or mist. Water may also be applied to the garden crops by means of a hose by running the water in furrows between the rows or by running the water in tile placed under the soil. The chief factor that must be considered in any system of irrigation is a sufficient supply of water.

CONTROL OF INSECTS AND DISEASES.

Preventive measures are best in the control of insects and diseases. (Fig. 34.) All old vines, cabbage stalks, and the remains of the various crops should be gathered and burned in the autumn. This destroys many insects and to a large measure will prevent the spread of diseases. Following each crop with something not related to it will aid in keeping down insects and diseases. The hand picking of such insects as the Colorado potato beetle is to be recommended. The use of air-slaked lime or dust as a deterrent for insects is effective and inexpensive. The control of garden insects and diseases is fully covered in Farmers' Bulletin 856, "Control of Diseases and Insect Enemies of the Home Vegetable Garden," to which the reader is referred for further information.

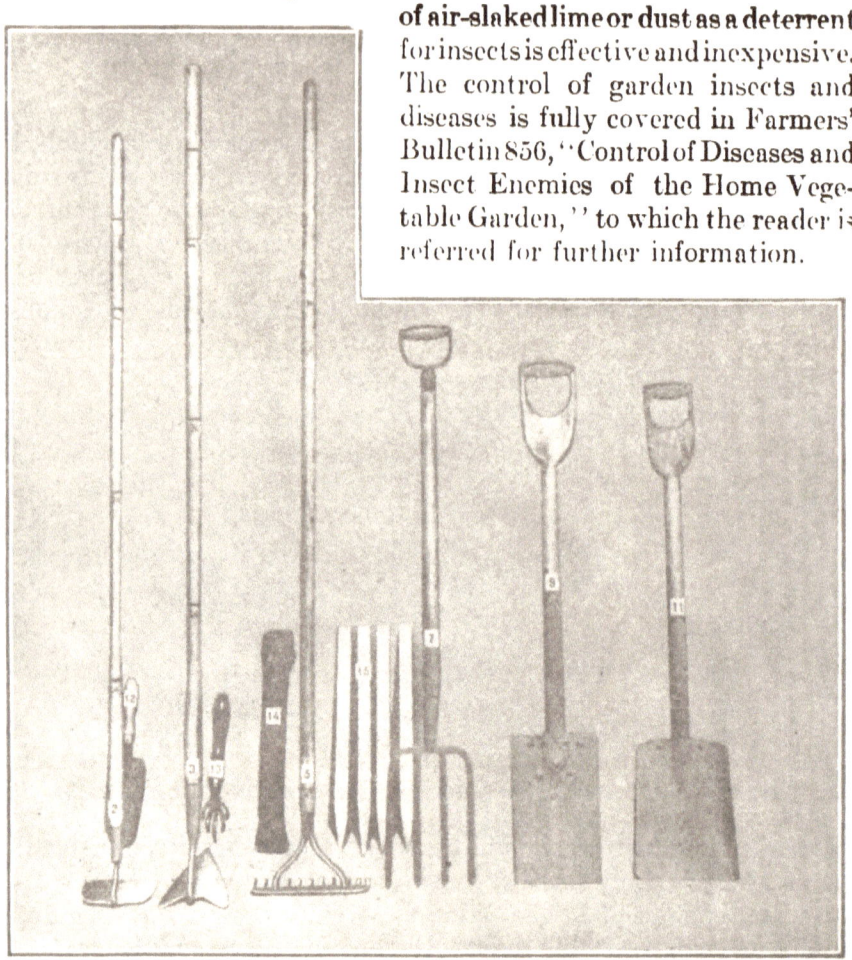

FIG. 28.—A set of garden tools, including the essential implements and a few others. (2) Hoe, (3) heart-shaped furrow hoe, (5) steel-tooth rake, (7) fork, (9) spade, (11) shovel, (12) trowel, (13) scratch weeder, (14) line, (15) stakes. Note that the handles of some of the longer implements are marked off in feet and half feet for convenience in measuring.

SAVING SURPLUS VEGETABLES.

It is just as important to utilize all surplus vegetables as it is to raise them. Those vegetables that are not needed when freshly harvested may be stored, canned, or dried for use during the months when few vegetables are available in the garden. Vegetables may be easily stored with the facilities in or near the ordinary home. Small pits (fig. 35) may be made in the ground, or a portion of the house cellar (fig. 36) may be partitioned off to serve as a storage cellar.

For details of the storage of vegetables, read Farmers' Bulletin 879, entitled "Home Storage of Vegetables."

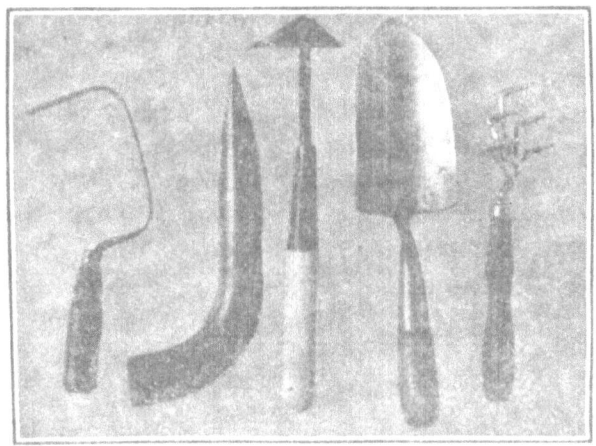

Fig. 29.—Some small tools useful in the home garden. From left to right they are: Hand weeder, dibble, onion hoe, trowel, and scratch or claw weeder.

Detailed directions for canning vegetables are to be found in Farmers' Bulletins 839[1] and 853[2] and for drying in Farmers' Bulletin 841.[3]

DIRECTIONS FOR GROWING VEGETABLE CROPS.

ASPARAGUS.

Asparagus should be grown in every home garden where it will thrive, because it is one of the earliest vegetables and is a valuable addition to the spring diet. The soil for asparagus should be made quite rich by the application of partly rotted manure before the plants are set. As soon as danger from hard frosts is over, the seeds of asparagus may be sown in the rows where the plants are to remain. Soaking the seed in hot water for an hour or two before planting will hasten germination.

The seedlings should be thinned to stand 15 inches apart in the row. Quicker results can be secured,

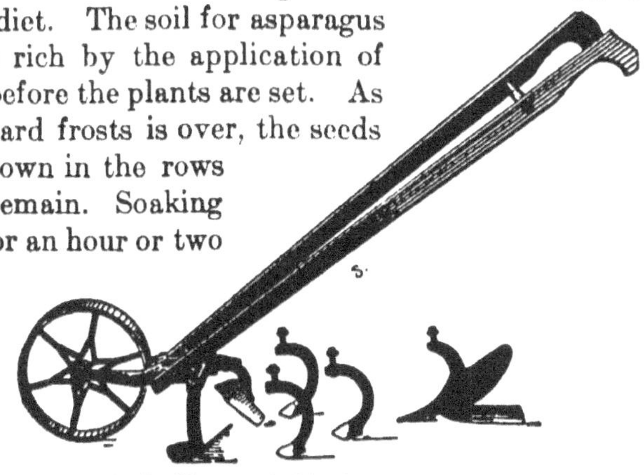

Fig. 30.—A wheel hoe, a valuable addition to any vegetable garden.

---

[1] Entitled "Home Canning by the One-Period Cold-Pack Method Taught to Canning Club Members in the Northern and Western States."

[2] Entitled "Home Canning of Fruits and Vegetables as Taught to Canning Club Members in the Southern States."

[3] Entitled "Drying Fruits and Vegetables in the Home, with Recipes for Cooking."

however, by buying roots from some seedsman or dealer. The roots may be planted in the autumn or early spring. Before setting the plants, the soil should be loosened deeply by spading or by the use of a subsoil plow. The roots may be set in a solid bed 1 foot apart each way. Cover the roots to the depth of 4 or 5 inches. The bed should receive a dressing of manure or fertilizer each year, preferably in the autumn.

No shoots should be removed the first year the plants are set in the permanent bed, and the cutting season should be short the second year. After the bed is well established, with proper care and fertilizing it should last indefinitely. During the cutting season, all of the shoots, even those too small for use, should be removed.

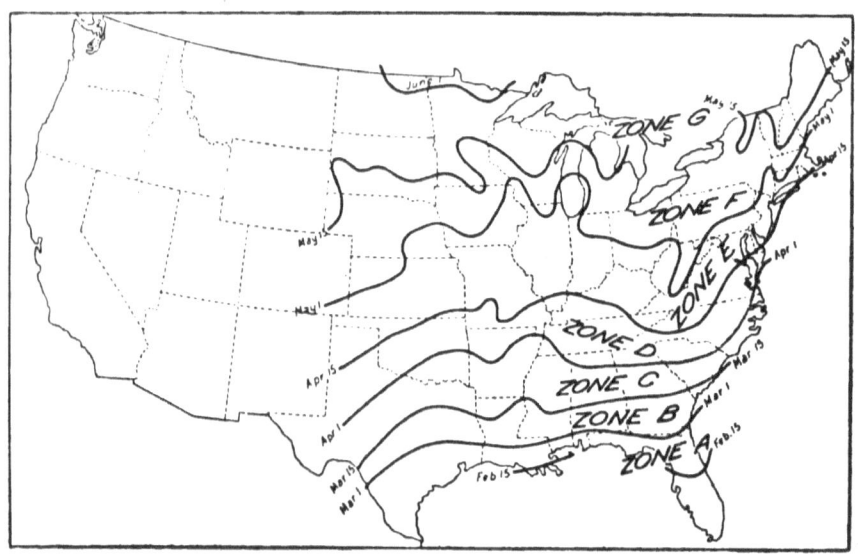

FIG. 31.—Outline map of the United States, showing zones based on the average date of the last killing frost in spring. The time of planting for the various vegetables is determined for every section by the dates given on this map.

After this, the tops should be allowed to grow until late in the season, when they should be removed and burned and the soil between the rows cultivated. Apply a dressing of manure after cultivation and allow it to remain on the bed.

Varieties recommended: Palmetto, Reading Giant, and Giant Argenteuil.

BEANS.

Beans will not withstand much cold, so they should not be planted until danger of frost is past and the ground begins to warm up. The first planting should be made as soon as the ground is reasonably warm, and other plantings may be made at intervals of ten days or two weeks until hot weather sets in. Beans for the fall garden should be planted in late summer, and successive plantings may be made at the intervals suggested until about eight weeks before time for the first frost in the autumn.

Bush beans should be planted to stand 2 to 3 inches apart in rows 20 to 24 inches apart. Among the best varieties of bush beans are the Stringless Green Pod, Refugee, Hodson's Kidney Wax, Currie's Rustproof Wax, and Wardwell's Kidney Wax.

Lima beans, both pole and bush, should be grown in the garden (fig. 37). These should be planted after all danger of frost is over and the soil is warm. Plant the pole beans 8 to 10 seeds in a hill and thin to 3 or 4 after the plants become established. The hills should be 4 or 5 feet apart. For bush Lima beans, plant 5 or 6 inches apart in rows 30 to 36 inches apart.

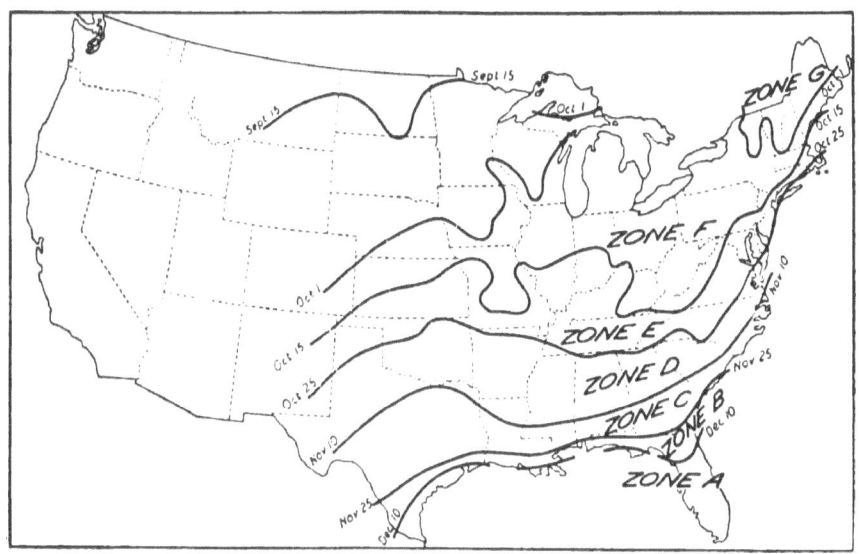

FIG. 32.—Outline map of the United States, showing zones based on the average date of the first killing frost in the autumn. The latest safe dates for planting vegetables in the autumn are determined by the dates given on this map.

When planting beans of any kind the seed should not be covered over 2 inches, and on heavy soils they should not be covered more than $1\frac{1}{4}$ to $1\frac{1}{2}$ inches.

Varieties recommended: Seibert's Pole Lima, Carpinteria Lima, and King of the Limas are good varieties of pole Lima beans, and Fordhook Bush Lima, Dreer's Bush Lima, and Henderson's Bush Lima are good varieties of the bush type.

BEETS.

Beets (fig. 38) can be planted as soon as the ground can be worked up mellow in the spring, even before the ground has become warm. Sow the seeds in drills 14 to 18 inches apart, covering to the depth of about 1 inch. As soon as the plants are well up, thin them to stand 4 to 5 inches apart. Make two or three plantings, so as to have a continuous supply of young, tender beets throughout the season. In many sections of the South beets may be left in the ground through the winter, to be pulled when wanted.

Varieties recommended: Crosby's Egyptian, Bassano, Early Eclipse, and Early Blood Turnip.

CABBAGE.

In Florida and the Gulf coast region of the other Southern States cabbage seed may be sown in the open any time from September to January. Along the Atlantic coast, from Charleston, S. C., to Florida, seed may be sown in the open in October. In all other sections of the South hotbeds or coldframes should be used for starting the plants.

For spring and early-summer cabbage the following varieties are recommended: Jersey Wakefield, Charleston Wakefield, Allhead Early, and Succession. The Copenhagen Market, a new variety, has given excellent results in many localities and is well worthy of a trial. The Flat Dutch and Danish Ball Head are desirable late varieties for the Northern States.

In most sections of the South it is not advisable to grow cabbage during midsummer, but a fall crop should be grown. The same varieties may be grown in the autumn as in the spring, but it is usually desirable to plant larger varieties, such as Flat Dutch or Danish Ball Head. Seed for the fall crop should be planted in a cool loca-

FIG. 33.—A poorly kept garden, involving a waste of time, energy, and seed.

tion in late summer and the plants set out as soon as they reach the proper size and the soil contains sufficient moisture to start growth. Cabbage plants should be set 14 to 18 inches apart in rows 30 to 36 inches apart. The earlier varieties, which grow small heads, are usually set closer than the later ones.

CARROT.

The soil and cultural requirements of carrots are practically the same as for beets. Carrot seed, however, should not be planted so deep as beet seed, and the plants can be allowed to grow closer together in the row (fig. 39). Carrots may be dug in the autumn and stored in banks or cellars, or they may be left in the ground to be harvested as needed.

Varieties recommended: Half-Long Danvers, Early Scarlet Horn, and Chantenay.

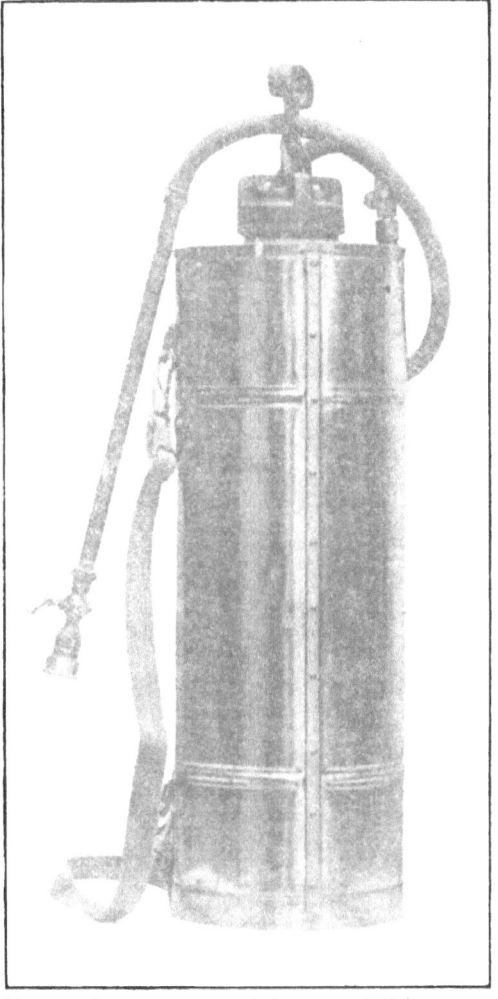

FIG. 34.—A type of compressed-air sprayer which is very useful in a home garden.

CAULIFLOWER.

Cauliflower thrives best on a rich, moist soil. The culture of this crop is about the same as for cabbage, but it will not withstand as much frost. In order to secure bleached heads it is necessary to protect them from the sun (fig. 40). The usual practice is to tie the leaves together over the heads.

Varieties recommended: Early Snowball and Dwarf Erfurt are the varieties of cauliflower most commonly grown.

CELERY.

In the lower South celery is grown as a fall crop, as it will not mature during hot weather. The seed is sown in a cool, shady place in late summer and the plants set out in the autumn as soon as the soil becomes moist. The seed should be sown in rows and covered lightly (not more than one-eighth of an inch) or sown broadcast and covered with burlap, straw, or some other material, to prevent the loss of moisture while the seed is germinating. It will be necessary to water the seed bed often during dry weather.

In the North or upper South celery may be grown in the spring or in the autumn. As a spring crop, the seed should be started in a hotbed during the winter so that the plants may mature before midsummer. Celery does not bleach well in hot weather, but rots when banked or boarded for bleaching.

Set the celery plants 6 inches apart in rows 3 feet apart for horse cultivation, or 18 to 24 inches apart when hand cultivation is to be employed.

Celery requires a deep, rich, moist soil and frequent shallow cultivation. When grown as a fall crop celery may be planted after some other crop, such as peas, beans, cabbage, lettuce, or radishes. When

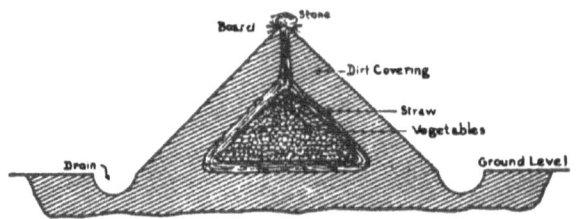

FIG. 35.—A method for the storage of root crops. Cross section of a storage pit containing Irish potatoes. During severely cold weather the dirt covering may be supplemented by manure, straw, etc.

the celery plants are nearly grown a little soil should be drawn around the base to hold the plants in place. About two weeks before they are wanted for the table the bleaching should begin. Soil, boards, or paper may be used for bleaching, but soil should be employed only when the weather is cool. When soil is to be used for bleaching, the rows should be 4 feet apart. Some quick-maturing crop could be grown between the rows of celery to make use of the space up to the time for bleaching.

Varieties recommended: Golden Self-Blanching, Columbia, and White Plume.

COLLARD.

A group of nonheading cabbages differing slightly from kale, but withstanding summer heat better than either kale or cabbage, is extensively grown throughout the South under the name of Georgia collards. Collards do not make a true head, but form a rosette of leaves, which are very tender. The culture and uses of this plant are the same as those of cabbage and kale.

CHARD, SWISS.

Swiss chard is a beet plant that has been developed for the foliage instead of for the root (see fig. 38). The leaves continue to develop throughout the season and are picked off when small. Two or three of the central shoots are always left to carry on the growth. Chard is planted like beets in rows 12 to 14 inches apart and gradually thinned out so the plants stand 12 inches apart in the row. The seed is sown at the same time as beets and the leaves are ready for use in about five weeks. The fleshy leafstalk is very often used the same as asparagus.

Swiss chard is especially useful in the small garden because the leaves can be used for greens in place of spinach and a sufficient number of plants occupy only a small fraction of the space needed to raise the required supply of spinach.

Giant Lucullus is the variety commonly grown.

CORN, SWEET.

Sweet corn should be planted on rich land and cultivated the same as field corn (fig. 41). Plant the seed as soon as the soil is warm in the spring, and make successive plantings every two or three weeks until late summer.

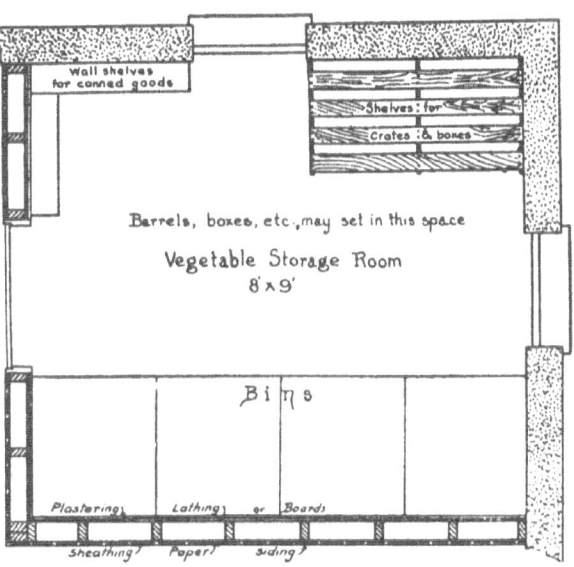

FIG. 36.—A plan showing how a storage room may be made in the cellar of a dwelling. The arrangement of the shelving and bins may be changed to suit conditions. While the construction of the wall may be varied, it must be tight.

The same results can be obtained to some extent by planting early, medium, and late varieties. Plant the seeds about 2 inches deep in drills 3 feet apart, and thin to a single stalk every 10 to 14 inches.

The flavor of sweet corn depends upon the stage of maturity and the method of handling the product from the plant to the table. Sweet corn loses its flavor very rapidly after being removed from the stalk. It should, therefore, be picked only a few hours, and preferably a few minutes, in advance of the time when it is to be placed in the pot.

Varieties recommended: For early corn Golden Bantam and Adams Early are suggested, and for medium and late varieties Black Mexican, Country Gentleman, and Stowell's Evergreen. The last-named variety has the largest ears and is the most productive.

Fig. 37.—A tennis backstop forming a good support for Lima beans. The yield from these vines was 25 quarts of shelled beans.

CUCUMBERS.

The soil for cucumbers should be rich, and it is a good plan to apply well-rotted manure under the rows or hills. If planted in rows, open the furrow and scatter the manure along the furrow, turning fresh soil over the manure before planting the seeds. If the seeds are planted in hills, confine the application of manure to the area occupied by the hills.

As cucumbers are easily injured by cold, it is not advisable to plant until all danger of frost is over and the ground has begun to warm up. For very early cucumbers the seeds should be planted in a hotbed in old strawberry boxes or plant bands or directly in the soil of the bed. By starting the plants in hotbeds the cucumbers will be ready for the table two or three weeks earlier than if started in the open. For the main crop, drill the seed in rows 5 feet apart, and after the plants reach a height of 3 or 4 inches thin them to stand 12 to 18 inches apart in the row, or plant the seeds in hills 4 feet apart each way and thin to two or three plants to the hill.

Cucumbers should be given frequent shallow cultivation until the vines fill most of the space between the rows; after this very little attention will be needed, except to pull out any weeds by hand. Do not allow any fruit to ripen on the vines until the end of the picking season, as new fruits will not form while older ones are ripening.

Young cucumber plants are often destroyed by the cucumber beetle. It is possible to protect the plants by covering them with small wooden frames over which mosquito netting has been stretched.

Air-slaked lime sprinkled over the small plants is an added protection against the cucumber beetle.

Varieties recommended: White Spine, Davis Perfect, and Emerald.

EGGPLANT.

The plants for this crop should be started in a hotbed or in a box in the house about two months before time for planting in the garden. The plants should not be set in the field until after all danger of frost has passed and the ground has become quite warm. Set the plants 18 to 24 inches apart in rows 3 feet apart, and give clean, shallow cultivation to keep the plants growing rapidly. A dozen good,

FIG. 38.—Beets and Swiss chard, excellent crops in any home garden.

healthy plants will supply enough fruit for the average-sized family throughout the season.

Varieties recommended: New York Improved Purple and Black Beauty.

GARLIC.

Garlic is propagated by separating the bulbs into the small bulblets, or cloves, and planting these separately in rows 12 to 14 inches apart and from 3 to 4 inches apart in the row, either in the autumn or spring. In other respects the cultivation is the same as for onions. The mature bulbs are pulled and left on the ground until the tops are dry, when they are gathered, braided together, and hung in a shed to cure. Garlic is used for flavoring purposes.

KALE.

Kale is a very hardy crop and can be grown in the open during the winter in practically all sections of the South. In the more northern sections it is grown either as a spring or fall crop. Sow the seed in

FIG. 39.—A patch of excellent carrots in a city garden.

drills 18 inches apart, and thin the plants to stand 4 or 6 inches apart in the row. Seed for the spring crop may be sown as soon as the soil can be conveniently worked. Seed for the fall or winter crop may be sown in early autumn.

Varieties recommended: Dwarf Curled, Tall Scotch, and Siberian.

KOHL-RABI.

Kohl-rabi belongs to the same class as cabbage and cauliflower, but does not resemble either. The edible portion is the swollen stem, which resembles a turnip, but which is formed above ground. Kohl-rabi should be grown both in the spring and in the autumn. Sow

FIG. 40.—A row of cauliflower in a vacant lot garden. The leaves are tied at the top to keep the heads white.

the seed in drills and thin the plants to 6 inches apart in the row. The rows should be 18 inches apart. The fleshy stems should be used while fresh and tender, as they become tough and stringy within a short time.

Variety recommended: White Vienna.

LETTUCE.

Lettuce thrives best during cool weather, so it should be planted in the spring and autumn. In order that the leaves or head may be crisp, the crop should be forced and successive plantings made ten days or two weeks apart. In the lower South lettuce can be grown in the open during the winter, but in the North hotbeds or coldframes must be used.

When grown in the garden, the seeds should be sown in rows 14 to 16 inches apart and the plants thinned to the desired distance. The heading type should be thinned to stand 8 inches apart in the row, but with the loose-leaf type the plants may be grown close together and thinned as needed for the table. For a very early crop, start the plants in the hotbed or coldframe and transplant the young plants to the garden as soon as hard freezes are over. Give the plants frequent shallow cultivations.

Varieties recommended: Grand Rapids and Black-Seeded Simpson for loose-leaf lettuce, and Big Boston, Hanson, and California Cream Butter for head lettuce.

MELONS.

Muskmelon.—The culture of the muskmelon is the same as for the cucumber, except that the plants are usually given more space. Plant 8 to 10 seeds in a hill, spacing the hills 6 feet apart each way After the plants become established, thin out all but four of the best ones. Another method is to sow in drills 6 feet apart and thin to single plants 18 to 24 inches apart.

FIG. 41.—Corn grown in a lot utilized as a home garden.

Varieties recommended: Rocky Ford, Netted Gem, Emerald Gem, Paul Rose, and Osage.

Watermelon.—The cultivation of the watermelon is the same as for the cucumber and muskmelon, except that the plants require more space. Plant watermelon seeds in rows 8 to 10 feet apart and thin to single plants 3 feet apart, or plant in hills 8 to 10 feet apart each way.

Varieties recommended: Kleckley Sweets, Florida Favorite, Georgia Rattlesnake, and Tom Watson.

MUSTARD.

Mustard is used largely for greens and can be grown in early spring and late autumn. The seeds for the spring crop should be sown as soon as the soil can be put into condition. For the fall crop, sow the seeds in the late summer or early autumn in drills about 1 foot apart. As the plants require but a short time in which to reach edible maturity, frequent sowings should be made.

Varieties recommended: Giant Ostrich Plume and Large-Leaved Curled.

OKRA, OR GUMBO.

Okra is a plant that is especially desirable in southern gardens. Sow seeds in the open after danger of frost is over and the soil becomes quite warm. The rows should be 3 to 4 feet apart for dwarf varieties and 4 to 5 feet for the tall kinds. Sow the seed a few inches apart in the row and thin the plants to 18 inches to 2 feet apart. Give frequent shallow cultivations until the plants are nearly grown.

The pods are the part of the plant used for food and should be gathered while still crisp and tender. If the pods are removed so as to allow none to ripen, the plants will continue to bear until killed by frost.

Varieties recommended: White Velvet, Dwarf Green Prolific, Perkins Mammoth, Long Podded, and Lady Finger.

ONIONS.

For very early bunch onions it is the common practice to plant sets in drills 12 to 14 inches apart and 2 to 3 inches apart in the row. In the South the sets may be put out in the autumn or as early in the spring as the land can be prepared. In the North the sets are put out as soon as the ground can be worked in the spring.

For dry onions, sow the seed thickly in drills about 12 to 14 inches apart in the spring as soon as danger from hard frosts is over. For early bulbs the seed may be planted in a hotbed or coldframe and the young plants transplanted to the open when conditions are favorable. Plants 4 or 5 inches high are of good size for transplanting.

Onions require frequent shallow cultivations and it may be necessary to resort to hand weeding. When the tops begin to die and the bulbs are full grown, the onions should be pulled and left in the field for a few days to dry. Then the tops should be clipped off and the bulbs placed in crates or bags and stored in a well-ventilated place to cure.

Early green onions may also be produced from the Multiplier or Potato varieties planted in the autumn. The large bulbs of these onions contain a number of "hearts", or buds, and if planted will produce a number of small onions. The small onions have but one heart and will produce large bulbs. A few large bulbs should be planted each year to produce sets for fall planting.

The Top, or Tree, onion produces a number of bulblets on top of the stem. These small bulbs can be planted in the autumn and will produce onions the following spring.

Varieties recommended: Southport White Globe, Southport Red Globe, Southport Yellow Globe, Danvers, Red Wethersfield, Australian Brown, and Prize Taker. In some sections of the South the Creole is grown and the Louisiana, or Red Creole, is a popular variety. The Bermuda is a good type of mild-flavored onion and is a desirable type to grow in the South. The important varieties of the Bermuda are Crystal Wax, White Bermuda, and Red Bermuda.

OYSTER PLANT. See SALSIFY.

PARSLEY.

Parsley is used mainly for garnishing meats, but can be used for flavoring soups and other foods. Sow parsley seed thickly in a drill or sow broadcast and cover lightly, either in the autumn or early spring. A space a yard square will be sufficient for parsley.

Varieties recommended: Plain Leaved and Double Curled.

PARSNIP.

Sow parsnip seed in the spring as soon as danger of hard frosts is over, in drills 14 to 16 inches apart. Thin the plants to stand 3 inches apart in the rows. The cultivation of parsnips should be about the same as for beets and carrots. A crop may be planted in midsummer for winter use, and the roots may be left in the ground through the winter or until needed, as freezing is believed to improve the flavor of parsnips. If it is desired to plow the garden before the parsnips are disposed of, they may be dug and stored in a cool place or buried in banks or pits.

Varieties recommended: Hollow Crown and Student.

PEAS.

Garden peas, sometimes called English peas, are not injured by light frosts, so they should be planted as soon as the soil can be put in order in the spring. The first plantings should be of small-growing, quick-maturing varieties, such as Alaska, First and Best, and Gradus, which do not require supports. These varieties should be followed by the large wrinkled type of peas, such as Champion of England, Telephone, and Prize Taker. The large-growing varieties should be supported on brush, on strings attached to stakes driven in the ground, or on wire netting. In order to have a continuous supply of peas, plantings should be made every 10 days or two weeks until warm weather. Peas should be planted in late summer and autumn for the fall garden, for which the early varieties are more desirable than the late ones.

Peas should be planted about 2 to 3 inches deep in rows 3 to 4 feet apart. Some gardeners, however, follow the practice of planting in double rows 6 inches apart, with the ordinary space of 3 to 4 feet between these pairs of rows. This is a good practice with varieties requiring support, as the supports can be placed in the narrow space between the rows.

Varieties recommended: Alaska, First and Best, Gradus, Telephone, Champion of England, and Prize Taker.

PEPPERS.

Seeds of peppers should be sown in a hotbed or in a box in the house about eight weeks before time for setting the plants in the garden. The plants are tender and should not be transplanted until the ground is warm and all danger of frost is past. Set the plants 15 to 18 inches apart in rows $2\frac{1}{2}$ to 3 feet apart. The cultivation and treatment of peppers should be the same as that of tomatoes and eggplants. There is a large number of varieties of peppers, including the sweet kinds and the hot peppers.

Varieties recommended: Ruby King, Chinese Giant, Sweet Spanish, and Bell or Bull Nose, of the sweet peppers; Long Red Cayenne, Tabasco, and Red Cluster, of the hot types.

POTATOES.

Irish or white potatoes.—A small area of early potatoes should be grown in the garden, but the main crop should be grown elsewhere. Early potatoes should be planted as soon as the ground can be prepared to good advantage. In Florida, potatoes are usually planted in December, while in other sections of the lower South they are planted in January. In the upper South early potatoes are usually planted in February, but in the Northern States they are not planted until March or April.

Potatoes are planted 12 to 14 inches apart in rows $2\frac{1}{2}$ to 3 feet apart and covered to the depth of about 4 inches. Potatoes planted during hot weather sohuld be covered 6 inches deep unless they have been sprouted before planting. The furrows are opened and the potatoes dropped, one piece in a place, in the bottom of the furrow. As it requires two or three weeks for potatoes to come up, it is important that they be cultivated as soon as the row can be followed. If a crust forms before the potatoes come up, a rake should be run over the ground to loosen the surface of the soil. Hand cultivators should be used for the main cultivation, but at the last cultivation the soil may be worked up around the plants to hold them erect and to protect the tubers from the sun.

After digging the early potatoes they should be kept in a cool, dry place during the hot weather of summer. In the South it is better to grow a fall crop rather than to try to keep the spring crop through the summer and winter. Fall-grown potatoes can be kept in a dry cellar, in a pit, or in any building where the temperature can be controlled. Irish potatoes keep best in a cool temperature, but should not be allowed to reach the freezing point. It is best not to allow the temperature to fall below 36° F.

Varieties recommended: Irish Cobbler, Bliss Red Triumph, and Early Rose are good, early potatoes. Where only one variety is to be grown, the Irish Cobbler is recommended. In the South the same varieties may be grown for the fall crop, or the Green Mountain, which is a late variety, may be used. In the North the Green Mountain and Rural New Yorker are commonly used for late varieties.

RADISH.

The radish is quite hardy and may be grown in the open all winter in the South and in coldframes in the North. Sow the seed in the open ground as soon as danger of hard frosts is over, or in coldframes whenever space is available. In the open, sow the seed in drills 12 to 15 inches apart and thin the plants to 1 inch apart. Successive plantings should be made every 10 days or two weeks until hot weather comes and again in the autumn when the weather begins to get cool.

Varieties recommended: There are three types of radishes—turnip shaped, olive shaped, and long. Of the turnip shaped, the best varieties are the Scarlet Globe and Scarlet Turnip. The best of the olive-shaped sorts are the French Breakfast and Early Scarlet. The Long Scarlet Chartier, Long White Spanish, and Icicle are the best varieties of the long type.

RHUBARB.

Rhubarb can be grown in the North and the upper South, but can not be grown satisfactorily in the lower South. For home use it is best to buy roots from a dealer rather than to grow plants from seed. Ten to twelve good hills are sufficient for the average family.

Set the roots 3 to 4 feet apart along the garden fence and manure heavily. The treatment suggested for asparagus is satisfactory for rhubarb. Do not allow the plants to go to seed.

SALSIFY, OR VEGETABLE OYSTER.

Sow seeds of salsify at the same time and in the same manner as those of parsnips and carrots. An ounce of seed will plant a 100-foot row and will be sufficient for an average family. After the plants are up, thin them to about 2 inches apart in the row. Salsify may be dug and stored the same as parsnips and carrots or left in the soil until needed. It is a biennial, and if the roots are not dug they will produce seed the second season. Salsify deserves more general cultivation, as it is one of the most desirable root crops.

The Sandwich Island is the variety commonly grown.

SPINACH.

Spinach is one of the best crops grown for greens and should be found in every large home garden. It can be grown in the open throughout the autumn and winter in all sections along the coast from Norfolk, Va., south and in the lower tier of Southern States. In the lower portions of the northern sections it requires protection during the coldest weather. Two or three inches of hay, straw, or leaves will be a satisfactory protection. The seed planted in the autumn will furnish greens through the winter and early spring in the warmer sections. In the Northern States the crop is usually grown in the spring.

Sow the seeds of spinach in drills 12 to 15 inches apart at the rate of 1 ounce to 100 feet of row. Three or four ounces of seed will produce enough greens for the average family. In gathering, the entire plant is removed. The large plants are selected first and the smaller or later ones are thus given room to develop.

The Savoy is the variety most commonly grown.

SQUASH.

There are two types of squashes, the bush varieties and the running varieties. The bush varieties should be planted in hills 4 feet apart each way and the running varieties 8 to 10 feet apart each way. Squashes are prolific, and the supply for the average family will ordinarily be furnished by five or six hills of each sort. Squash seed should not be planted until after danger of frost is over and the soil is quite warm. The cultivation and care of squashes should be the same as that given cucumbers or muskmelons.

Varieties recommended: The varieties of summer squash commonly grown are Pattypan, Summer Crookneck, and Vegetable Marrow. Of the winter squashes the Hubbard and Golden Hubbard are among the best.

TOMATOES.

To get a crop of early tomatoes the seed should be started about eight weeks before time for setting the plants in the field. In the South the plants can be grown in coldframes covered with canvas or cotton cloth, but in the North a hotbed should be employed. When only a few plants are needed the seed may be sown in a shallow box in the house. For the best results in growing tomatoes the young plants should be transplanted as soon as they reach a height of 1½ to 2 inches. Transplant them to stand 2 inches apart each way in a hotbed, coldframe, or box in the house. When the plants begin to crowd, it is a good plan to transplant them to flower pots, plant bands, old strawberry boxes, or tin cans from which the bottoms and tops have been melted.

Tomato plants should be set in the open as soon as danger of frost has passed. If the plants are to be pruned to one or two stems and tied to stakes, they should be set 18 inches apart in rows 3 feet apart. If the plants are not pruned or staked, they may be planted 3 feet apart in rows 4 feet apart. It is advisable, however, to prune and train to stakes, especially for the early crop, as plants so treated will be healthier and more easily cultivated and will produce fruit which is earlier and more uniform in size and shape than that produced by plants which have not been trained and pruned. Soon after setting the plants in the field a stake should be driven near each plant, to which it may be tied. Care should be exercised to tie the plant so that it will not be injured by the string. A good plan is to loop the string around the stake and tie it under a leaf stem. Go over the patch once every week or ten days and remove all shoots starting in the axils of the leaves.

Varieties recommended: For early tomatoes, Earliana or Chalk's Early Jewel is recommended, preferably the former. For medium and late varieties, the following are suggested: Greater Baltimore, Red Rock, Globe, Beauty, Acme, and Stone. The Stone is usually preferred for canning.

TURNIPS.

The turnip should be grown both as a spring and as a fall crop. For the spring crop, plant as early as the condition of the soil will permit, and for the fall crop sow the seed in late summer or early autumn. Sow the seed thickly in rows 15 to 18 inches apart, and as the plants reach a height of 4 or 5 inches begin thinning, using the young plants for greens. For good roots thin the plants to about 3 inches apart in the row. Cultivate turnips the same as carrots and parsnips. Turnips may be left in the ground until needed for the table, pulled and stored in a cellar, or buried in banks or pits.

Varieties recommended: Purple-Top Globe, White Globe, Seven Top, White Milan, and Yellow Aberdeen.

Rutabaga.—Rutabagas may be grown as a fall and winter crop to very good advantage. They are planted the same as turnips, except that they require more room and a longer period of growth.

The Purple Top is the most common variety of rutabaga.

U. S. DEPARTMENT OF AGRICULTURE
FARMERS' BULLETIN No. 1044

THE CITY HOME GARDEN

FRESH VEGETABLES for an average family may be grown upon a large back yard or city lot.

The use of fresh vegetables adds variety to the diet and improves the health of the people.

The production of vegetables at home relieves transportation difficulties and solves the marketing problem.

The city home garden utilizes idle land and spare time for food production.

Thousands of acres of idle land that may be used for gardens are still available within the boundaries of our large cities.

Some of the problems that confront the city gardener are more difficult than those connected with the farm garden, and it is the object of this bulletin to discuss these problems from a practical standpoint.

Washington, D. C. Issued March, 1919; revised June, 1930

THE CITY HOME GARDEN

By W. R. BEATTIE, *Senior Horticulturist, Office of Horticultural Crops and Diseases, Bureau of Plant Industry*

CONTENTS

	Page		Page
Type and location of the city garden	1	Crops for the city home garden	17
Preparation of the soil	3	Beans	18
Use of ashes on garden soils	5	Root crops	19
Liming garden soils	6	Tomatoes	22
Use of manure on garden land	6	Sweet peppers	23
Commercial fertilizers	7	Eggplant	24
Tools	8	Okra, or gumbo	24
Seeds	8	Onions	25
Starting early plants	8	Cabbage group	26
Planting zones	12	Greens and salad plants	27
General care of the garden	16	Vegetables that require considerable space in the garden	29
Holding moisture	16		
Watering	16	Vine group	31
Diseases and insects	17		

THE PROBLEMS that confront the city gardener are vastly greater than those of the farmer, who is free to select the choicest plot of ground upon the farm for his vegetable garden. The city-lot or back-yard garden as a rule offers little choice of soil or location. The available land is often shaded a part of the day, and the soil frequently consists of hard clay or is covered to a depth of several inches with cinders, broken stone, or other materials unfit for growing plants. The city gardener is usually handicapped by lack of practical experience and for want of suitable tools with which to do the work. Hand methods must be employed for the most part, and numerous local difficulties must be overcome. It is possible, however, to grow certain kinds of vegetables under very adverse conditions, and the results obtained by many city gardeners are truly remarkable.

The city back-yard or vacant-lot garden provides a supply of vegetables at home without transportation or handling costs. Vegetables from the home garden are fresher and more palatable than those brought from a distance. Many persons who work in offices, stores, and factories have time mornings and evenings that may well be devoted to the cultivation of a garden, thus utilizing spare time and idle land for food production. The home vegetable garden should be a family interest, and all members of the family who are able to do so should take part in its cultivation. There is no better form of outdoor exercise than moderate working in the home garden, and few lines of recreational work will give greater returns for the time employed. (Fig. 1.)

TYPE AND LOCATION OF THE CITY GARDEN

There are three general types of city vegetable gardens: Back-yard gardens, vacant-lot gardens, and community gardens. In locating the home garden the back yard or the grounds surrounding the dwelling should be given first consideration, because of the convenience both in working the garden and in gathering the products as wanted for use. If the grounds around the dwelling are too small or too densely shaded, or if the soil is of such a character that vegetables can not be grown successfully upon it, the use of a vacant lot in the neighborhood is recommended. (Fig. 2.) Community gardens located in the outskirts of the city, where a tract of land can be secured, are adapted for the use of families living in apartment houses; also for shopworkers and persons employed by large manufacturing concerns. There is a distinct advantage in having the garden located near the home, as much of the work of tending it may be done during spare moments, and the garden can be protected from theft or from injury by stray animals.

Do not locate the garden on land upon which the sun does not shine for at least five hours each bright day. Do not locate the garden on soil where the rock is but a few inches below the surface and where there is insufficient moisture. Do not attempt to grow a garden where a fill has been made with cinders or broken bricks or where the original soil has been buried with materials upon

FIGURE 1.—Small back-yard gardens in a residence section of Washington, D. C.

which weeds will not grow. If weeds grow rank and vigorous it is a sure sign that the soil is good. Do not plant a garden under or near large trees that will steal all the moisture and plant food from the crops. The maples and the oaks are the kinds of trees that are most injurious to crops planted near them. Do not plant a garden on low land where the crops are reasonably sure to be lost from overflow. Failure to observe one or more of these precautions has resulted in disappointment on the part of many gardeners.

Where there is any choice in the selection of a garden location the following points should be considered. The land should be level or gently sloping toward the south or southeast. The drainage should be good, but the land should not be so steep as to wash during rains. The location should be higher than adjoining land, in order to safeguard against frost, as frost does most damage on the lower levels. The ideal soil is a dark sandy loam with a rather retentive subsoil. The soil should be deep and should break up loose and mellow when plowed or spaded. Plenty of organic matter or rotted manure should be present in the soil, in order to give it the power to retain large quantities of moisture and to carry the crops through periods of drought.

The ideal garden spot is seldom found, but it is often possible to choose a location that embodies a number of the more important conditions and then supply others. The difficulties of the first season are greater than those of subsequent years, and a garden plot if properly handled will improve with each season's cultivation.

On account of the wide variety of local conditions that must be met, no definite plan can be given for a garden. A plan should be drawn on paper and the location of each crop decided upon. As a general rule, the rows should run north and south, but it is more

FIGURE 2.—A vacant-lot garden on one of the principal residence streets of Washington, D. C.

important to have the rows run the long way of the garden for convenience in cultivating. Figure 3 shows a well-planned garden.

It is essential that the garden be so arranged that the tall-growing crops will not shade the smaller ones.

PREPARATION OF THE SOIL

With the location of the garden settled, the first step is the preparation of the soil. First, remove anything that would interfere with the plowing or spading of the soil. If the location is the home back yard it is assumed that the ground is free from débris and ready to be broken up. If the garden is to be located on a vacant lot it is probable that there will be stones, broken bricks, tin cans, and other trash to be gotten rid of. If the quantity of trash is not too great it should be hauled to some dump, but if there is so much of it as to make its removal expensive it may be piled on one side or one end of the lot. In some cases stone fences have been built along the outside of lots from the stones that were scattered over the ground.

This cleaning-up process requires considerable work and should be done whenever the weather will permit prior to preparation for planting.

The next step in the garden-making process will be to plow or spade the ground. If the land is in sod it should be turned in the fall so that the sods will rot. Heavy clay soils should be turned up loosely and allowed to lie exposed to the freezing and thawing of

FIGURE 3.—Long straight rows of vegetables which add attractiveness to a garden and lessen the labor of cultivation. Note how this garden has produced these results

the winter months. In all cases manure should be turned under if it can be secured. If the surface soil is so hard that it can not be spaded or plowed to advantage a pick or a mattock should be used and the ground broken to a depth of 8 or 10 inches. Plenty of manure is about the only thing that will bring a soil of this character into condition. The supply of manure in cities is now quite limited, and the city gardener should make arrangements early in the season to get what he needs. It is assumed that the average back-yard garden is about 30 by 60 feet in size. About 1 ton of stable manure can be spaded into the soil of a plot of this size each year. On soil which has not been worked before and which is especially heavy and wanting in organic matter a larger quantity of manure can be used. Street sweepings are not desirable, as they frequently contain considerable oil. Sawdust and planing-mill shavings should not be used on garden land. Leaves may be mixed with heavy soils, but it is best to have them fairly well rotted before they are applied to the land.

Early breaking and exposure to frost is the best method of getting land that has not been under cultivation for a number of years in shape for planting. Sandy soils do not benefit by freezing and thawing as do the heavy clay soils, and in all cases precautions must be taken so that the soil will not wash away during heavy rains. It is a very good plan to plow or spade the land in the autumn, sow rye upon it, and then turn the rye under early in the spring.

In regions where the soil is very sandy it is often necessary to keep the surface covered with coarse manure or with some material to prevent it from blowing away. If this precaution is not taken the entire surface soil will be blown off to the depth of the plowing. In the spring the coarser part of the covering should be raked off before pulverizing and fitting the surface for planting.

Nothing is gained by working the land before it is sufficiently dry in the spring. In sections where the ground freezes hard during winter no harm will be done by plowing it in the fall or during the early winter when quite wet, as the freezing will correct any injury; but land that is worked when too wet in the spring will be injured for the entire season. The usual test is to press a small quantity of the soil in the palm of the hand. If it is too wet for working it will adhere in a solid mass and retain the imprint of the hand, but if dry enough to work it will crumble apart of itself.

When the test shows its fitness for working, land that was plowed or spaded in the fall should be thoroughly harrowed, raked, hoed, or forked over to a depth of 4 or 5 inches, in order to fit it for planting. The more carefully this part of the work is done the easier it will be to care for the crops during the growing season. Land that was not worked in the fall should be plowed or spaded as soon as it dries out sufficiently in the spring, and the top should be thoroughly fitted, as previously suggested.

USE OF ASHES ON GARDEN SOILS

Gardeners frequently ask whether it is advisable to use coal and wood ashes on garden soils. The use of coal ashes on heavy clay soils will tend to lighten them, but the ashes should be screened before they are applied, in order to remove any clinkers or cinders. They should then be spread evenly upon the land and thoroughly mixed with it. Coal ashes have little value as a fertilizer, their use being mainly to loosen the soil and make it more workable.

Wood ashes that are produced by the burning of hardwoods, such as oak and hickory, frequently contain as much as 7 per cent of potash and also a little lime, and for this reason are a valuable fertilizer. Wood ashes produced by the burning of pine and other softwoods, and hardwood ashes that have been exposed to the weather and have had their potash leached from them, have comparatively little value as a fertilizer. Not more than 50 pounds of reasonably dry unleached hardwood ashes should be applied to a plot of ground 30 by 60 feet in size, and these should be well mixed with the soil.

LIMING GARDEN SOILS

Lime improves the texture of certain heavy soils, but its excessive use may prove injurious to most garden crops. As a general rule asparagus, celery, beets, spinach, and sometimes carrots are benefited by the moderate use of lime, especially on soils that are naturally deficient in lime. Most of the garden vegetables do best on soils that are slightly acid, and all vegetables are injured by the application of lime in excess of their requirements. For this reason it should be applied only where it is definitely shown by actual test to be necessary, and in no case should it be applied in large quantities. As a matter of fact most garden soils that are in a high state of fertility do not require the addition of lime. With good drainage, plenty of manure in the soil, and the moderate use of commercial fertilizers, the growth requirements of nearly all vegetables may be fully met.

Where lime is applied it should be spread following plowing and should be well mixed with the topsoil by harrowing. (Fig. 4.) It should not be applied at the same time as, or mixed with, commercial fertilizers or manure, on account of the chemical changes that take place resulting in the loss of nitrogen, and thus destroying the effectiveness of the fertilizers. Lime should not, as a rule, be applied in the fall, on account of its becoming leached from the soil during the winter. Any of the various forms of lime such as hydrated lime and air-slaked lime may be used. In some cases the unburned but finely ground limerock is used, but its action is slower than that of the burned lime. Finely ground oyster shells and marl are frequently used as a substitute for lime. Lime should not be used on land that is being planted to potatoes because of its influence on the development of potato scab.

USE OF MANURE ON GARDEN LAND

The use of barnyard manure on garden land has already been mentioned, but too much stress can not be placed upon this important point. The most successful commercial gardeners not only follow the practice of plowing or spading under large quantities of manure, but they stack up manure to rot and apply the rotted manure as a top-dressing when fitting the land for planting. Beans, tomatoes, and potatoes may be injured by the use of too much manure, but it is practically impossible to have the land too rich for most garden crops.

Poultry and pigeon manures are excellent fertilizers for the garden, but must be used sparingly as they are very strong and are liable to burn the crops. These manures should be kept under shelter until used and then should be well mixed with the soil, care being taken that no lumps of the manure come in direct contact with the seeds. Not more than 200 pounds of poultry or pigeon manure should be applied to a garden plot 30 by 60 feet in size.

Sheep manure is sold by florists and seedsmen and is an excellent fertilizer for garden crops. Like poultry manure, it is very strong and should be used sparingly. A little pulverized sheep manure sprinkled along the rows and worked into the soil will give the plants a vigorous growth.

COMMERCIAL FERTILIZERS

The use of commercial fertilizers is advisable, especially where plenty of stable or barnyard manure can not be procured. As a rule, fertilizers should be sown broadcast and thoroughly harrowed or raked into the upper 3 inches of soil. Where applied underneath the rows the fertilizer should be well mixed with the soil before the seeds are planted. Great care must be taken in the use of commercial fertilizers in a small garden, as there is always a tendency to use too much and thereby do more injury than good. From 40 to 60 pounds of a standard fertilizer, such as is used by truck gardeners, may be applied to a plot of ground 30 to 60 feet in size. A fertilizer containing about 5 per cent nitrogen, 8 per cent phosphoric acid,

FIGURE 4.—Applying lime to a garden after plowing and before harrowing

and 5 per cent potash or one containing about 7 per cent nitrogen, 6 per cent phosphoric acid, and 5 per cent potash is good.

Commercial fertilizers may be used in very moderate quantities as a side dressing for most growing crops. Nitrate of soda is frequently used in this manner, especially with crops that are grown for their leaf and stem development rather than for fruit. Where used as a side dressing it is best to apply the fertilizer a short distance from the plants but where the small feeder roots will reach it. The fertilizer should be worked into the soil immediately.

It should be remembered that the best results are obtained by the use of commercial fertilizers where there is plenty of manure or organic matter in the soil. All sods and weeds and the remains of garden plants that are not infected with disease should be turned under or composted in one corner of the garden, in order to form material with which to enrich the soil.

TOOLS

Elaborate or expensive tools are not necessary for the cultivation of a small garden; in fact, a spade or a spading fork, a hoe, a steel rake, and a line with two stakes to fasten it to are all that are required. A garden trowel and a watering can may be added to advantage but are not absolutely necessary. A wheelbarrow, a wheel cultivator, and a seed drill are desirable for the larger gardens and might be procured and used jointly by several gardeners in a neighborhood. After the soil is broken and in shape for planting, the hoe and the steel rake are the important tools for a small garden.

SEEDS

A comparatively small quantity of seeds is required for planting the average city garden, but these should be procured in ample time and should be of the highest quality obtainable. The best are the cheapest in the long run. Garden seeds should not be wasted; only enough should be planted to insure a perfect stand. Any seeds that are left over should be stored in a ventilated tin or glass container, to protect them from mice until needed for later planting.

The particular variety of any crop to plant will depend upon local conditions. There are usually experienced persons in each community who can be relied upon for advice as to the best varieties to plant in that section. A number of the seed houses offer special garden seed collections adapted to various conditions and sizes of gardens.

STARTING EARLY PLANTS

Half the pleasure and profit of a garden is derived from having something to use just as early in the spring as possible. In many cities and towns each year the local greenhouse men grow thousands of plants which are sold to home gardeners at very reasonable prices. It often happens, however, that home gardeners do not have the opportunity to purchase well-grown plants, so they must start their own supply of early plants in the house or in a hotbed if they desire to have their crop mature early. Among the garden crops that may be started to advantage in this manner are tomatoes, early cabbage, peppers, eggplant, and lettuce. Even cucumbers, melons, squashes, beets, snap beans, Lima beans, and sweet corn may be started indoors by using flowerpots, paper bands, or berry boxes to hold the soil. Early southern-grown plants of cabbage, tomato, pepper, and onion are now being used extensively by northern gardeners.

Where just a few tomato and cabbage plants are desired, the seeds may be sown in a cigar box or in a shallow tin pan with a few holes punched in the bottom for drainage. A very good plan is to secure a soap box and saw off about 3 inches of the bottom portion to form a tray. If the top has been saved it can be nailed on and the box again sawed, forming a second tray. Any shallow box (fig. 5) that may be fitted into the window of a living room where there is a reasonable amount of sunlight will answer for starting early plants.

After filling the trays with sifted soil, smooth off even with the top and slightly firm down the soil in the trays by means of a small piece of board. Use the edge of a ruler or a strip of thin board (fig. 6) to form little grooves or furrows in the soil in which to plant

FIGURE 5.—Window box for starting early plants in the house.

FIGURE 6.—Starting early plants; preparing the seed box

the seeds. These little rows should be about 2 inches apart and one-fourth inch deep. Scatter the seeds of tomato, early cabbage, pepper, and eggplant, as shown in Figure 7, very thinly in the rows, and cover them by sifting a small quantity of soil over the entire surface. Smooth the top of the soil gently and water very lightly.

The box should then be placed where the temperature will remain at about 70° F. If conditions are kept right, the seedlings will appear in five to eight days after the seed is planted. From this time on the plants will need constant care, especially as regards watering. Owing to the fact that the light from a window comes from one side only, the seedlings will draw toward the glass, and the box should be turned each day so as to keep the plants from growing crooked. Just as soon as the little plants are large enough to handle they should be transplanted to other boxes and given 2 or 3 inches of space in each direction.

Where the required number of plants is too great for growing in window boxes, a hotbed or a coldframe may be provided. The usual method of constructing a hotbed is first to dig a shallow pit

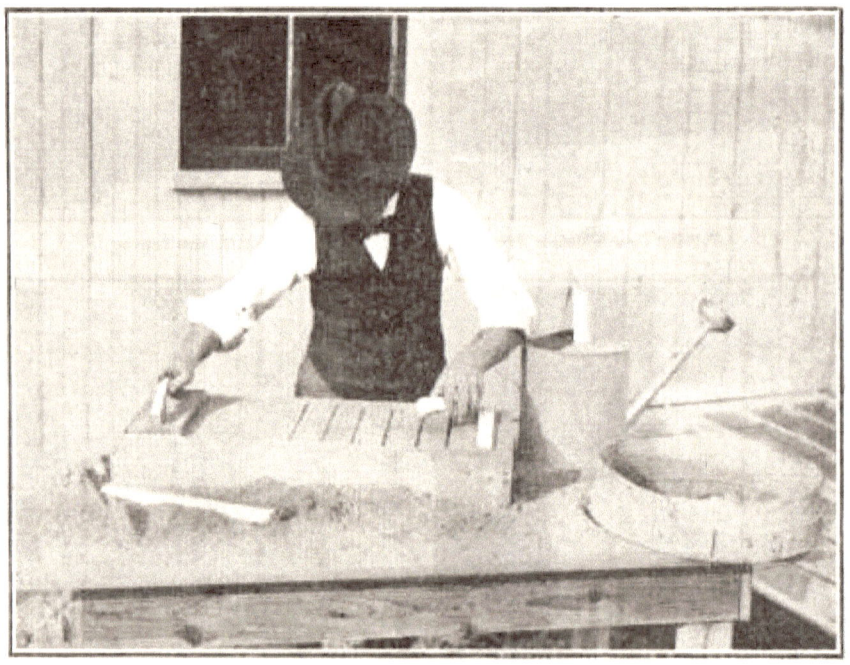

FIGURE 7.—Starting early plants; sowing seed in the window box

8 to 18 inches deep, according to locality, and pack it full of fermenting stable manure. The manure before being placed in the pit should be turned over once or twice in a pile in order to insure even heating. It may then be packed into the hotbed pit and tramped uniformly. Standard hotbed sash are 3 feet in width and 6 feet in length, and the size of the bed should be made to suit the number of sash employed. A framework of boards 18 to 24 inches high at the back and about 12 inches high in front is placed over the manure-filled pit to support the sash. (Fig. 8.)

About 3 or 4 inches of fine garden loam is spread evenly over the manure, and the bed is allowed to stand four or five days to warm up before any seed is sown. At first the temperature of the bed will run rather high, and it is best to delay planting the seeds in it until it begins to decline. This can best be determined by placing a thermometer with the bulb about 3 inches below the surface of the soil and watching it until the temperature falls below 85° F. before planting the seeds.

If glazed sash are not available for covering the hotbed, heavy muslin may be used instead; the glass, however, makes the most desirable form of covering. Care must be taken to give the bed sufficient ventilation to prevent overheating, as it is liable to heat up rapidly when the sun shines full upon the glass. Watering should be done during the early part of the day and the bed given enough air so that the plants will dry off before night. The bed should be closed before evening, in order to conserve enough heat to carry it through the night in good condition. If the weather should turn severely cold, a covering of straw, blankets, or canvas may be thrown over the bed to protect it.

A coldframe is constructed in exactly the same manner as a hotbed, with the exception that no manure is placed beneath it to supply heat.

FIGURE 8.—Preparation of a sash-covered frame for starting early plants

Before the plants are set in the garden, from either the hotbed or the coldframe, they should be gradually hardened to outside conditions by giving them more ventilation each day. Finally, remove the sash entirely on bright days and replace them for the night. The aim should be to produce strong healthy plants that will make a quick start when placed in the garden.

PLANTING ZONES

Tables 1 and 2, together with the frost-zone maps (figs. 9 and 10), are based upon records of the United States Weather Bureau covering a period of 20 years and are intended to serve as a guide for determining the earliest dates that the various garden crops may be planted in the spring, also the latest dates that it will be safe to plant certain crops and have them mature before the first killing frost in the autumn. It should be borne in mind that there is a difference of several days in the frost occurrence within each zone; this is due to differences in altitude and latitude and also to the proximity of bodies of water and large tracts of timber.

Owing to the varied character of the Rocky Mountain and Pacific coast regions, it is not practical to present the planting information in zone form, as there may be a very great difference in the dates of killing frosts in the same general locality, on account of ele-

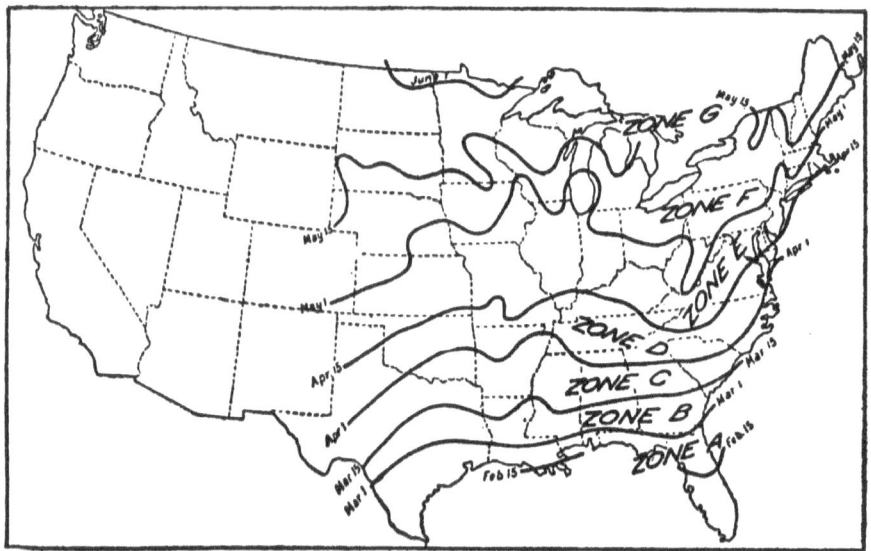

FIGURE 9.—Outline map of the United States, showing zones based on the average date of the last killing frost in spring. The time of planting for the various vegetables is determined for each section by the dates given on this map

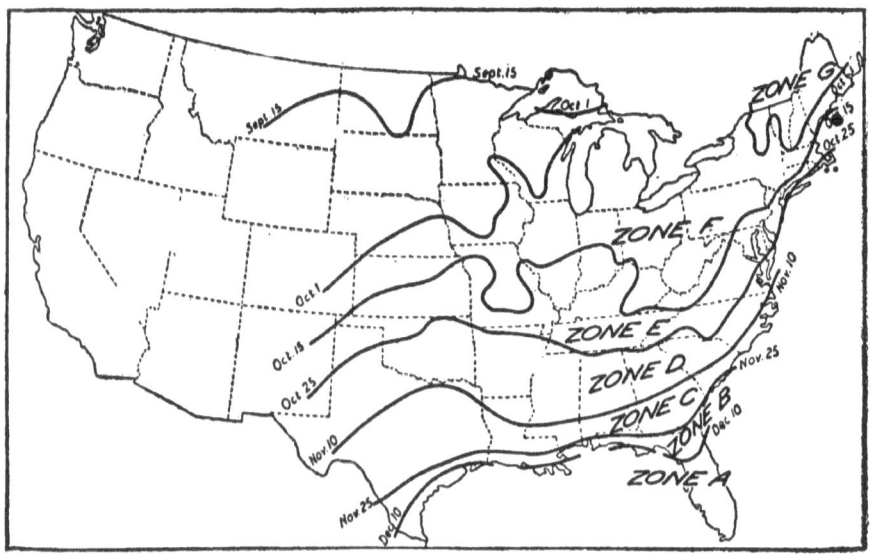

FIGURE 10.—Outline map of the United States, showing zones based on the average date of the first killing frost in the autumn. The latest safe dates for planting vegetables in the autumn are determined by the dates given on this map

vation. Gardeners on the Pacific coast should be guided by the experience of competent persons in their own neighborhood. The coast region of Oregon and Washington is so influenced by ocean currents that a separate map would have to be designed to meet its requirements.

TABLE 1.—*Earliest safe dates for planting vegetables in the open in the zones shown in Figure 9*

Crop	Zone A	Zone B	Zone C	Zone D	Zone E	Zone F	Zone G
Bean:							
Lima	Mar. 1 to 15	Mar. 15 to Apr. 1	Apr. 1 to 15	May 1 to 15	May 15 to June 1	May 15 to June 1	May 15 to June 15.
Snap	Feb. 15 to Mar. 1	Mar. 1 to 15	Mar. 15 to 30	Apr. 1 to May 1	May 1 to 15	May 15 to June 1	May 15 to June 1.
Beet	Feb. 1 to 15	Feb. 15 to Mar. 1	Mar. 1 to 15	Mar. 15 to Apr. 15	Apr. 15 to May 1	May 1 to 15	Do.
Brussels sprouts	do	do	do	do	do	do	May 1 to 15.
Cabbage	Jan. 1 to Feb. 1	Jan. 15 to Feb. 15	Feb. 15 to Mar. 1	Mar. 1 to 15	Mar. 15 to Apr. 15	Apr. 15 to May 1	May 1 to June 1.
Carrot	Feb. 1 to 15	Feb. 15 to Mar. 1	Mar. 1 to 15	Mar. 15 to Apr. 15	Apr. 15 to May 1	May 1 to 15	Do.
Cauliflower	do	do	do	do	do	do	Do.
Celery	do	do	do	do	do	do	Do.
Chard, Swiss	do	do	do	do	do	do	Do.
Collard	Jan. 1 to Feb. 1	Feb. 1 to 15	Feb. 15 to Mar. 1	Mar. 1 to 15	Mar. 15 to Apr. 15	May 1 to June 1	May 15 to June 15.
Corn, sweet	Feb. 15 to Mar. 1	Mar. 1 to 15	Mar. 15 to Apr. 1	Apr. 1 to May 1	Apr. 15 to May 15	May 15 to June 15	June 1 to 15.
Cucumber	Mar. 1 to 15	Mar. 15 to Apr. 1	Apr. 1 to 15	Apr. 15 to May 1	May 1 to June 1	do	
Eggplant	do	do	do	do	do	do	May 15 to June 1.
Kale	Jan. 1 to Feb. 1	Feb. 1 to 15	Feb. 15 to Mar. 1	Mar. 15 to Apr. 1	Apr. 15 to May 1	Apr. 15 to May 1	May 1 to 15.
Kohlrabi	Feb. 1 to 15	Feb. 15 to Mar. 1	Mar. 1 to 15	Mar. 15 to Apr. 1	May 1 to 15	May 1 to 15	May 15 to June 1.
Lettuce:							
Head	do	do	do	Mar. 15 to Apr. 15	Mar. 15 to Apr. 15	do	Do.
Leaf	do	Feb. 1 to 15	Feb. 15 to Mar. 1	Mar. 1 to 15	Mar. 15 to Apr. 15	Apr. 15 to May 1	May 1 to 15.
Melon	Mar. 1 to 15	Mar. 15 to Apr. 1	Apr. 1 to 15	Apr. 15 to May 1	May 1 to June 1	June 1 to 15	
Okra, or gumbo	Feb. 15 to Mar. 1	Mar. 1 to 15	Mar. 15 to 30	May 1 to 15	May 1 to 15	May 15 to June 1	
Onion sets	Jan. 1 to Feb. 1	Feb. 1 to 15	Feb. 15 to Mar. 1	Mar. 1 to 15	Mar. 15 to Apr. 15	Apr. 1 to May 1	May 15 to June 1.
Parsley	Feb. 1 to 15	Feb. 15 to Mar. 1	Mar. 1 to 15	Mar. 15 to Apr. 1	Apr. 1 to May 1	May 1 to 15	Do.
Parsnip	do	do	do	do	do	do	
Pea:							
Smooth	Jan. 1 to Feb. 1	Feb. 1 to 15	Feb. 15 to Mar. 1	Mar. 15 to Apr. 15	Mar. 15 to Apr. 15	Apr. 15 to May 1	May 1 to June 1.
Wrinkled	Feb. 1 to 15	Feb. 15 to Mar. 1	Mar. 1 to 15	Mar. 15 to Apr. 15	Mar. 15 to Apr. 15	May 1 to 15	May 15 to June 1.
Pepper	Mar. 1 to 15	Mar. 15 to Apr. 1	Apr. 1 to 15	Apr. 15 to May 1	Apr. 15 to May 15	June 1 to 15	May 1 to June 1.
Potato	Jan. 1 to Feb. 1	Feb. 1 to 15	Feb. 15 to Mar. 1	Mar. 1 to 15	Mar. 15 to Apr. 15	Apr. 15 to May 1	May 1 to June 1.
Pumpkin	Mar. 1 to 15	Mar. 15 to Apr. 1	Apr. 1 to 15	Apr. 15 to May 1	May 1 to 15	June 1 to 15	
Radish	Jan. 1 to Feb. 1	Feb. 1 to 15	Feb. 15 to Mar. 1	Mar. 1 to 15	Apr. 15 to May 1	Apr. 15 to May 1	May 1 to 15.
Salsify	Feb. 1 to 15	Feb. 15 to Mar. 1	Mar. 1 to 15	Mar. 15 to Apr. 1	Apr. 15 to May 1	May 1 to 15	May 15 to June 1.
Spinach	do	Feb. 1 to 15	do	do	Mar. 15 to Apr. 15	Apr. 15 to May 15	Do.
Squash	do	do	Apr. 1 to 15	Apr. 15 to May 1	May 1 to June 1	June 1 to 15	
Sweetpotato	Mar. 1 to 15	Mar. 15 to Apr. 1	do	do	do	May 15 to June 15	June 1 to 15.
Tomato	do	do	do	do	do	do	
Turnip	Jan. 1 to Feb. 1	Feb. 1 to 15	Feb. 15 to Mar. 1	Mar. 1 to 15	Mar. 15 to Apr. 15	Apr. 15 to May 1	May 1 to 15.

TABLE 2.—*Latest safe dates for planting vegetables for the fall garden in the zones[1] shown in Figure 9*

Crop	Zone C	Zone D	Zone E	Zone F	Zone G
Bean:					
Pole Lima	Sept. 15	Aug. 1	July 15	July 1	
Snap	---do----	Sept. 1	Aug. 15	Aug. 1	July 15
Beet	---do----	---do----	---do----	---do----	Do.
Cabbage	Sept. 1	Aug. 15	July 15	July 1	June 15
Carrot	---do----	---do----	---do----	---do----	Do.
Cauliflower	---do----	---do----	---do----	---do----	Do.
Celery	Oct. 1	Sept. 1	Aug. 1	---do----	May 15
Chard, Swiss	Sept. 15	---do----	Aug. 15	Aug. 1	July 15
Corn, sweet	Aug. 15	Aug. 1	July 15	July 1	June 15
Cucumber	---do----	---do----	---do----	---do----	
Eggplant	July 15	July 1	June 15	June 1	
Kale	Nov. 1	Oct. 1	Sept. 15	Sept. 1	Aug. 15
Lettuce	---do----	---do----	Sept. 1	Aug. 15	Aug. 1
Melon:					
Muskmelon	July 1	July 1	June 15		
Watermelon	June 15	June 1	May 15	May 1	
Okra	July 15	July 1	June 15	June 1	
Onion sets	---do----	---do----	---do----	---do----	May 15
Parsley	Nov. 1	Oct. 1	Sept. 1	Aug. 1	July 1
Parsnip			May 15	May 1	Apr. 15
Pea	Nov. 1	Oct. 1	Sept. 1	Aug. 1	July 15
Pepper	July 15	July 1	June 15	June 1	
Potato	Aug. 15	Aug. 1	July 15	July 1	June 15
Radish	Oct. 15	Oct. 1	Sept. 15	Sept. 1	Aug. 15
Salsify	June 15	June 1	May 15	May 1	Apr. 15
Spinach	Oct. 15	Oct. 1	Sept. 1	Aug. 15	Aug. 1
Squash:					
Bush	Aug. 15	Aug. 1	July 15	July 1	June 15
Vine	July 15	July 1	June 15	June 1	
Sweetpotato	Aug. 15	July 15	---do----	May 1	
Tomato	---do----	---do----	July 1	June 15	
Turnip	Oct. 15	Oct. 1	Sept. 1	Aug. 1	July 15

[1] Zones A and B are sections in which many vegetables are planted late in the fall to form the winter garden or early spring garden.

In zones A, B, C, and parts of zone D of the eastern United States, cabbage, turnip, spinach, kale, collard, and certain varieties of onion may be grown in the open ground throughout the winter. In certain parts of zone E spinach and kale may be grown all winter. In zone F such crops as sweetpotato, melons, eggplant, and peppers should be planted only under the most favorable conditions, as the season is sometimes too short for their full development under adverse conditions.

Garden plants are divided into about four more or less distinct groups.

Early cabbage, kale, onion sets, peas, potatoes, spinach, and radishes may be planted two weeks before the average date of the last killing frost.

Beets, Swiss chard, carrots, lettuce, peas, cauliflower, and sweet corn may be planted about the date of the last killing frost.

Beans, parsnips, salsify, melons, cucumbers, tomatoes, and sweetpotato plants may be planted after the last killing frost.

The heat-loving plants, such as peppers, eggplant, Lima beans, and the squashes, should not be planted in the open until the ground has thoroughly warmed, which will be two to four weeks after the last killing frost.

There are a number of crops, such as snap beans, lettuce, radishes, and beets, that should be planted at intervals in order to insure a continuous supply throughout the season. In the case of snap beans as many as five different plantings may be had in some sections. In the southern part of the United States special attention should be given to the planting of the semihardy crops, such as spinach, kale, and cabbage, during the autumn, in order to have a supply throughout the winter.

By following the planting dates given in Table 2 (see also fig. 10), the various crops will mature during average years; however, there may be seasons when the first killing frost in the autumn occurs earlier than usual and some of the later plantings will be lost. The late planting of vegetables prolongs the season of usefulness and is worth a chance.

GENERAL CARE OF THE GARDEN

A garden bears close acquaintance, and the successful gardener is the one who keeps in close contact with his crops throughout the entire growing season. A visit to the garden during the early morning while the dew hangs heavily upon every plant will reveal the happenings of the night. Perhaps some insect attack has started or some injury has occurred which requires immediate attention. A garden requires a little attention almost every day and responds in direct proportion to the care bestowed upon it. The size of the garden should be such that its care will not prove a burden. A small garden intensively cultivated is much better than a larger one which is allowed to grow to weeds.

HOLDING MOISTURE

The frequent stirring of the surface soil with a steel rake will stimulate the growth of the crops and control weeds. The surface should be stirred after a rain just as soon as the ground is dry enough to work. The stirring of the soil is primarily in order to kill weeds, but there is need of maintaining a loose friable condition and avoiding packing of the soil even where no weeds are present. The roots of plants require air as well as moisture, and frequent stirring of the surface soil admits the air and at the same time conserves moisture. Shallow cultivation during dry weather forms what is known as a soil mulch, preventing the escape of moisture.

WATERING

Artificial watering, if properly applied, will prove a decided advantage during dry periods, but may prove an injury if not properly done. Frequent light sprinkling of the garden is injurious. The proper method is to soak the soil thoroughly about once each week, preferably during the evening, and then loosen the surface by cultivation as soon as the soil is dry enough to work. No more water should be applied until absolutely necessary; then another soaking should be given. On a small scale the water may be applied by means of a sprinkling can. Where available, a garden hose is effective, and overhead sprinkler systems are frequently employed to advantage. Perhaps the best method for applying the water is to open slight furrows alongside the rows of plants and allow the water to flow gently along these furrows.

After the water has all soaked into the soil the wet earth in the furrows should be covered with dry soil to prevent baking. Where seeds are to be sown during a period of drought a slight furrow may be opened and filled with water; then, after the water has soaked into the soil, the seeds may be sown and covered with dry earth. This method will insure a good stand of plants, as the moisture feeds upward in the soil, like the oil in a lamp wick.

DISEASES AND INSECTS

Garden crops are subject to attack by a number of insects and diseases. Preventive measures are best, but if an attack occurs and the city gardener is not familiar with the insect or disease and the proper treatment to protect his crops he is advised to consult the local garden leader or write immediately to the Extension Division of the State College of Agriculture. The United States Department of Agriculture has bulletins containing the necessary information on garden insects and diseases, and these can be procured free upon request.[1]

Small compressed-air sprayers that may be carried by a strap over the shoulder of the operator are very satisfactory for use in the small garden. One of these sprayers will serve for several gardeners in a single neighborhood, and the original cost is reasonable. Wherever poisons are used in the fight against garden insects great care must be taken to see that they are stored in a safe place where there will be no chance of persons or animals becoming poisoned. Garden products such as snap beans should not be sprayed or dusted with poisons after the edible portions form.

Poisons may be applied in powdered form to a number of the garden crops, including potatoes, by means of a small burlap or cheesecloth bag, the poison being dusted upon the plants when they have dew upon them. This can be done in the morning before the plants have dried or late in the evening after the dew has begun to form.

CROPS FOR THE CITY HOME GARDEN

As a rule not more than 10 or 12 different kinds of vegetables should be grown in the city home garden. These should be chosen from the standpoint of securing the greatest food value from a limited area. Certain of the very important food crops, such as potatoes, peas, and sweet corn, require too much space for the small city garden, but should be included wherever the available space will permit.

Owing to the extreme variation of local conditions, no definite plan can be given for the city home garden, and each gardener will have to select the crops to be grown according to his soil, space, and the requirements of his family. By careful planning and by keeping every foot of garden space fully occupied a great quantity of produce can be secured from a comparatively small plot of ground. A succession of plantings of certain vegetables will produce a continuous supply, while others may be grown between the main crops, thus making the land do double duty. There is a tendency on the part of many persons to plant too heavily to lettuce and radishes. As a matter of fact a supply of these vegetables can be grown in the rows between the plants or hills of other crops. Most beginners attempt too many varieties and kinds of vegetables. They would do better

---

[1] For additional information on the insects and diseases of garden vegetables, see Farmers' Bulletin 1371, Diseases and Insects of Garden Vegetables.

to confine themselves to a few standard sorts, leaving the novelties to those who have plenty of land at their disposal.

It is assumed that the average space available for the city vegetable garden will not exceed 30 by 60 feet. Many gardens in back yards are smaller, while others located on vacant lots may include one-fourth acre or more. The size of the garden will determine largely the crops to be grown. The following cultural directions are based on average conditions and are subject to some modification to suit the locality.

BEANS

The bean crop stands at the head of the list in importance for the city garden, especially from the standpoint of producing a large quantity of food quickly on a limited space. The food value of the bean, in all forms, is also very high, and it may be grown under a wide range of conditions.

String beans, or snap beans in bush form, are the most popular for planting in the small garden. The seed should not be planted until the ground is fairly warm and the danger of frost safely passed. Stringless Green-Pod, Bountiful, Currie Rustproof Wax, and Refugee Wax are the leading early varieties of bush beans. Where space is limited the bush varieties can be planted in rows 24 inches apart, with the individual plants 3 or 4 inches apart in the row. Three or even four plantings at intervals of two or three weeks should be made, in order to insure a continuous supply. In sections where the first autumn frost does not occur until about the 1st of October a late or fall crop of snap beans can be grown to advantage, the seed being planted about the first week in August.

A half pint of seed of snap beans will plant about 100 feet of row with four seeds to a hill and the hills 12 inches apart. A hundred feet of row will be sufficient for one planting to supply the average family. If four plantings are made 1 quart of seed will be required.

Pole or climbing beans should be planted in every garden where space will permit. The variety known as Kentucky Wonder produces a plentiful supply that can be eaten pod and all while they are tender, as shelled beans when more mature, and as dry beans after they ripen. Pole or climbing Lima beans are adapted to a wide range of territory and can often be grown on a division fence, on a trellis covering the kitchen porch, or on an outbuilding. Figure 11 shows a street fence which is being made to support a fine crop of Lima beans. Bush Lima beans are less particular in their soil and climatic requirements, but are considered by many persons to be of finer quality than the pole varieties.

Lima beans require a richer soil than string or snap beans, and the seed should not be planted until the ground is quite warm, fully a week later than snap beans. All beans should be planted comparatively shallow, especially on clay or heavy soils. On light or sandy soils beans may be covered from $1\frac{1}{4}$ to 2 inches. Beans will not start well if planted in wet soil or if covered too deeply.

In case the soil should become packed by heavy rains before the plants appear, it is a good plan to break the crust over the row by means of a steel rake, great care being taken that the rake teeth do not go deep enough to injure the sprouting beans. Beans should not be worked when their leaves are wet with dew or rain, as this has a tendency to spread disease.

In case more beans are grown than are required for summer use, the young, tender pods may be canned for winter. Any beans that become too old for immediate use should be allowed to ripen and be saved for planting the next season or for cooking as dry beans. Colored dry beans are as good as white, both in flavor and nutritive value, in spite of a rather general popular belief to the contrary, and none of them should be wasted.

ROOT CROPS

The root crops, including beets, carrots, parsnips, salsify, turnips, and radishes, form a group of very important food crops for the small garden. The soil requirements and general culture are very much the same for all the root crops, and for that reason they are considered collectively. The soil for root crops should be quite

FIGURE 11.—Lima beans growing on the outside of a garden fence

rich, and it should also be spaded or plowed deep and made fine and mellow the full depth that is broken. These root crops will all withstand slight frosts and may be planted very early in the spring. Root crops are especially desirable for the small garden on account of the fact that the rows may be as close together as 12 or 14 inches and the plants 3 or 4 inches apart in the row, making it possible to grow a large quantity of food on a small area.

BEETS

An ounce of beet seed will be sufficient for the ordinary city garden. Beets may be planted almost as soon as the ground can be worked in the spring. Make the soil fine and mellow, then lay off the row about 1 inch deep, using the rounded end of the hoe handle to make the little furrow. What are commonly called beet seeds are really fruits each containing two or three seeds, and for that reason too many should not be put in. Eight or ten to the foot of row are sufficient. Cover the seeds about 1 inch and rake the surface smooth over the row. If the seeds are good and the weather favorable the plants should appear in about 10 days after planting. They should be thinned to about 3 inches in the row, but if not too thick to start with they may be allowed to reach a height of about 3 or 4 inches before thinning, and the thinnings may be used for beet greens. Any skips or spaces can be filled in by transplanting plants that are removed from other parts of the row. A row 50 feet long will furnish enough early beets to supply the ordinary family. A second planting may be made about four weeks after the first. A late planting should be made about six or eight weeks before the first autumn frosts. Any beets that are left in the garden at the end of the season should be stored for winter use.

Crosby's Egyptian and Detroit Dark Red are considered among the best varieties for the home garden.

CARROTS

One-fourth ounce of carrot seed will be more than enough to plant 50 feet of row early in the spring and to make another similar planting later for fall use and storage. Plant the seeds rather thickly, 15 or 20 to the foot, and cover them with about half an inch of light soil, but not more than one-fourth of an inch in heavy soil. Thin to 2 or $2\frac{1}{2}$ inches in the row as soon as they are large enough to handle. If desired, the plants may be left a little closer, then thinned a second time when the first of the young carrots are about half an inch in diameter. The young carrots that are thinned out may be used on the table as creamed baby carrots and are very fine. Late-planted carrots may remain in the ground until after the first frosts of autumn and then dug, topped, and stored in moist sand for winter use.

Oxheart, Chantenay, and Danvers Half-Long are common varieties.

PARSNIPS

A 10-cent packet, or about one-eighth of an ounce, of parsnip seed will be sufficient to plant for the ordinary family. Be sure that the seed is fresh, as it loses its vitality if kept over until the second year. Plant the same as carrots and thin to 3 or 4 inches in the row. Parsnips require a deeply prepared and very rich soil for their best development.

Parsnips may remain in the ground where grown during the winter or until wanted. It may be best, however, to dig part of the roots late in the fall before the ground freezes and store them for winter use.

In the North parsnips are planted quite early and given the entire season to develop and are used mainly during the winter and spring. In the South they may be planted quite early and used as a spring vegetable, and then another planting made for a fall crop. The later planting is usually made in August or September, when the late summer rains occur.

Hollow Crown and Guernsey are among the best varieties.

SALSIFY, OR VEGETABLE OYSTER

Salsify requires practically the same cultural treatment as parsnips. It is not grown extensively in the home gardens of the Southern States, but is primarily a northern crop. Salsify may remain in the ground during the winter, or a part may be dug late in the fall and stored in a bed or box of moist sand for winter use.

The Sandwich Island is the leading variety.

TURNIPS

Throughout the Northern States turnips are planted as a late-season crop, the seed being sown from July 10 to August 1 and the crop harvested after the first heavy frosts. In the Southern States turnips are planted in the spring, just as soon as the ground can be worked, and the crop is used before the hot weather of summer comes on. A late crop is frequently planted in September, the roots being cooked in the usual manner, while the young tender tops are boiled as greens.

For the small garden, turnips had best be planted in drills, with the rows about 12 inches apart, and the plants should be thinned to 2 or 2½ inches in the row. The seed should be scattered very thinly in the drill and covered very lightly. The plants removed in thinning may be used as greens. Turnips will withstand some frost, but their keeping qualities are injured if they are allowed to freeze before pulling. If they become frozen in the storage pit they should not be disturbed until the weather warms and they gradually thaw out. For best results turnips should not actually freeze at any time.

The Purple-Top Strap-Leaved is a leading variety.

RADISHES

Everybody wants a few early radishes in the garden, because they come to maturity quickly and furnish something green and succulent for the table. From 10 to 20 feet of row will produce all the radishes required by a family. The seeds should be sown in a little furrow or drill, about 12 or 15 seeds to the foot, and covered 1 inch. Radishes may also be sown thinly in the drill with beets, carrots, or parsnips, as they come quickly and break the surface for the other seedlings. The radishes should be pulled before they are large enough to injure the crop with which they are sown.

Scarlet Globe White-Tipped, French Breakfast, Icicle, and Long Scarlet Short Top are among the leading varieties.

Where it is desirable to have radishes for a considerable period of time, two or even three plantings at intervals of two weeks should be made, or the same result may be attained by the proper selection of varieties. There are also varieties of winter radishes that may be planted late in the summer for winter use. Long Black Spanish and China Rose are large, firm, pungent sorts.

TOMATOES

Tomatoes are among the most universally used products of our home gardens, and there should be a few plants, no matter how small the garden. In order to have tomatoes early, the seeds must be sown in the house or hotbed or the plants purchased from some plant grower who has the facilities for starting them early. Bonny Best,

Earliana, Acme, and Early Detroit are among the leading early sorts, while Marglobe and Stone are standard intermediate and late varieties. Two small packets of seed, one of an early and one of a late variety, will produce enough plants for several family gardens, and it may be possible for one person to start the plants for an entire neighborhood. If a window box is used for starting early plants of various kinds, a portion of the space in this box should be used for the tomato plants. Where a window box is not in use a cigar box filled with loose soil will serve as a seed bed, but the plants will have to be transplanted and given about 3 inches of space both ways as soon as they form one or two true leaves in addition to their two small seed leaves. Tomato seed comes up in about 8 to 10 days, and the seedlings will ordinarily be ready for transplanting in 2 weeks after the seed is sown. About 6 to 8 weeks will be required for growing the plants from the time of sowing the seed until they are ready for setting in the garden.

A tray of fine, rich soil about 3 inches deep placed in a south window of a living room makes a good transplanting bed. The plants can be grown in quart berry boxes, in 3-inch flowerpots, or in paper bands. The essentials are to keep the plants growing rapidly from the start and to retain all the dirt attached to their roots when setting them in the garden.

The best method of growing tomatoes in the small home garden is by pruning the plants to a single stem, or at most to two stems, and tying them to stakes or a trellis, as shown in Figure 12. By this method the plants can be set as close as 2 feet apart in each direction. When tied to stakes the plants are easy to cultivate. The fruit is clean because it is kept off the ground, and the tomatoes ripen earlier than when the plants are not pruned or tied to stakes. Any stakes that are about $1\frac{1}{2}$ inches in diameter and 4 to 5 feet long will answer. Frequently the plants are trained to horizontal wires stretched on small posts or to a trellis made of laths.

The tomato plants are pruned by pinching out the side shoots (fig. 12) as they appear in the axil of the leaf; that is, where it joins the main stem. The fruit clusters appear on the opposite side of the stem where there is no leaf. The plants are tied to the stakes or other support by means of soft twine or with small strips of old cotton goods. (Fig. 13.) Jute string is especially suitable for tying tomatoes. Loop the string around the stake so that it will not slip downward on the stake, and then tie loosely below a leaf node in such a manner that the stem will be supported without the string binding it and injuring its growth.

Four to seven fruit clusters will be formed on each plant, and if the plants are well cultivated and cared for they will continue to bear fruit throughout the season in the northern parts of the country. In the South, where the heat of midsummer kills tomato plants, a late crop may be planted for fall use.

SWEET PEPPERS

Sweet peppers are increasing in favor with home gardeners everywhere. Six or eight good plants will supply enough for an ordinary family. In the North, where the growing season is short, the plants must be started indoors and should be transplanted twice, so as to be quite large by the time the weather is warm enough to set them in the garden. Pepper plants will not withstand any frost, and they should not be set out until all danger is past. In the South the seed should be sown in the house or in a hotbed, and the young plants may be transplanted directly from the seed bed to the garden, although better plants will be obtained if they are transplanted first from the seed bed to other boxes or to the hotbed and later to the garden. The plants should be handled in the same manner as tomatoes, but pepper plants are even more delicate.

The Ruby King, California Wonder, World Beater, and Chinese Giant are standard varieties of the large sweet peppers. Pimento

FIGURE 12.—Training tomatoes to stakes: *A*, Cutting out the side shoots or branches; *B*, tying the main stem to the supporting stake

peppers are becoming very popular throughout the Southern States; however, they will not mature where the frost-free growing season is less than four and one-half months, and they are not profitable unless they have at least five months of warm weather for their development. The pimento is adapted to the South, where the summers are long, with plenty of hot weather. The green pimento peppers have a thick flesh and a pleasant flavor and may be used like any sweet pepper. When red ripe the pimentos are canned for winter salads and for mixing with cheese to make pimento cheese.

EGGPLANT

The seeds of eggplant should be sown indoors at the same time that early tomatoes and peppers are planted. The small plants should be transplanted to pots or paper bands and kept in the house until the weather is quite warm. The plants require a rich, deep soil, with plenty of fertilizer. They should be set about 3 feet apart each way. Five or six plants will be sufficient to supply the average family.

OKRA, OR GUMBO

Okra is sown in the open after danger of frost is over and the soil has become quite warm, but in the North a few plants for the home garden may be started indoors, like tomatoes or peppers. Sow the seed a few inches apart in the row and thin the plants to 18 inches to

FIGURE 13.—Tomatoes trained to stakes in a back yard garden

2 feet apart. Okra is very prolific, and 8 to 10 feet of row will supply the needs of an average family. Give frequent shallow cultivation until the plants are nearly grown.

The pods are the part of the plant used for food and should be gathered while still crisp and tender. If the pods are removed so as to allow none to ripen, the plants will continue to bear until killed by frost.

The White Velvet, Dwarf Green Prolific, Perkins Mammoth, Long-Podded, and Lady Finger varieties are recommended.

ONIONS

The usual method of growing onions in the home garden is to plant a quart or two of sets just as early in the spring as the ground can be worked. Throughout the South the sets may be planted in the autumn and the surface of the ground mulched with fine straw or light manure over the winter. Onions may also be grown from seed, sown in the early autumn in the South and in the early spring in the North, but as a rule it is more satisfactory to secure a few sets for planting.

Onions require a light, mellow, rich soil. If planted in rows the sets (fig. 14) should be placed by hand, root end downward, about 3 inches apart in the row and covered to a depth of 1 inch. If planted in a bed they should be spaced 4 to 6 inches apart in each direction. As a rule, onion sets are not sold under variety names, but are classed as white, brown, red, or yellow.

FIGURE 14.—Planting onion sets; every bulb is placed with the root end downward at a uniform depth and in straight rows

Southern-grown onion plants are frequently employed for planting in home gardens. These plants are a little less expensive than sets and usually produce a better grade of mature or keeping onion. They should be planted in rows 12 to 18 inches apart, with the plants 3 to 4 inches apart in the rows.

The Yellow Globe, Yellow Danvers, Red Wethersfield, and Silverskin are among the leading varieties that are planted from seed. The Crystal Wax and Red Bermuda varieties of the Bermuda type are often grown in the Southern States.

Where wanted for green onions, the sets may be planted as a filler in the rows with other early crops, but where mature onions are desired it is best to plant them alone. Fully grown onions should not be pulled until the tops have broken over and partially ripened.

The bulbs should then be pulled and spread in a cool, dry place where they will get plenty of air. The mature onions should be kept where it is quite cool and dry.

CABBAGE GROUP

The cabbage group includes both the early and the late types of cabbage, cauliflower, broccoli, kale, collards, Brussels sprouts, and kohlrabi. The general cultivation of each member of this group is practically the same, and they may be grown in almost any locality; in fact, cabbage is one of the most universally grown of our garden crops. The important consideration is to have plenty of plant food in the soil so that they will make a quick, tender growth.

EARLY CABBAGE

Only a few heads of early cabbage should be grown in a small city garden. The plants should be started indoors, but may be set in the garden quite early if hardened off a little before setting them. In certain sections of the South the early varieties of cabbage may be planted in the fall and matured the following spring. The Jersey Wakefield, Charleston Wakefield, Golden Acre, Glory of Enkhuisen, and Copenhagen Market are the leading early varieties. They may be set in rows 24 to 30 inches apart and 15 inches apart in the row.

LATE CABBAGE

Late cabbage can be planted between the rows of early potatoes or after early snap beans, so that double service may be obtained from the soil. All Seasons and Danish Baldhead are among the best late varieties. They should be planted in rows 30 inches apart and 18 inches apart in the row. Cabbage may be stored in a cool, dry, well-ventilated cellar or buried in an outdoor pit in the garden.

CAULIFLOWER

Cauliflower is much more difficult to grow than cabbage and is only adapted to certain soil and climatic conditions which are to be found near the seacoast and in limited inland areas. The important consideration in growing a spring crop of cauliflower is to have it so early that the heads will be formed before the extremely hot weather begins. The methods of starting the plants and general culture are the same as for early cabbage. When the heads begin to form, the leaves should be brought together above the heads and fastened by means of a string, so as to shut out the sunlight and retain the snowy whiteness of the heads. A fall crop of cauliflower can be grown in the same manner as late cabbage. Cauliflower can not be stored to advantage, but should be used within a few days after it is gathered.

KALE

Kale can be grown either as a spring or a fall crop, and in sections where the temperature does not go below zero during the winter it can be planted in the fall and will be ready for use during March and April. The market gardeners around Norfolk, Va., grow great fields of winter kale, planting the seed in September and cutting the crop at any time during the winter when the ground is free from snow and ice. About 50 or 60 feet of row in the home garden may be planted during the late summer for fall and winter use. Kale is not stored, but is left growing until wanted for use.

COLLARDS

No southern garden would be quite complete without a small plot of collards for late fall and early winter use. Collards are a hardy form of cabbage which produce a cluster of very tender leaves that are used in much the same manner as cabbage. Throughout the South collards are planted during the latter part of the summer and the plants are left standing where grown, like late cabbage, and are quite hardy; in fact, it is claimed that the flavor is greatly improved by a slight freezing. Collards are not recommended for planting in the Northern States. A small packet of seeds is all that is necessary to start the plants required in a family garden.

BRUSSELS SPROUTS

Brussels sprouts are a kind of cabbage that forms a large number of buttons or small heads along its stem where the leaves are attached. The culture of Brussels sprouts is the same as that of cabbage except that the leaves are removed from the lower part of the stem to give the buttons more room to develop.

KOHLRABI

Kohlrabi is a near relative of cabbage. It forms an enlargement of the stem just above the surface of the ground. This portion is used in the same way as turnips.

GREENS AND SALAD PLANTS

As a general rule, the American people do not eat enough green vegetables, commonly referred to as salads. Crops of this class are especially adapted to the small garden, as they occupy very little space and will withstand more or less shading. The salad plants require a deep, rich soil, with plenty of moisture. They also thrive under comparatively cool conditions.

SWISS CHARD

Swiss chard resembles the common garden beet in appearance, but it does not form an edible root, like the beet, and is grown for its large leaves, which are boiled for greens. Beet tops while young and tender make good greens, but the leaves of Swiss chard have a very excellent flavor and remain tender a long time. As the outer leaves are removed the plants keep on forming new leaves in the center, so that a continuous supply is provided.

Swiss chard is planted and cultivated the same as garden beets. One-half ounce of seed will be sufficient for the ordinary family of five persons. The variety known as Lucullus is considered best. Plant in the early spring the same as beets, and thin the plants to about 6 inches in the row.

SPINACH

Spinach thrives in cool weather and should be grown both as a spring and as a fall crop. In the extreme northern part of the country only one crop may be grown. In sections where the winters are mild the seed can be planted in the fall and the plants can remain in the ground all winter. For a spring crop, plant in the open ground as soon as the soil can be worked. The rows may be as close as 7 inches, and 12 to 15 seeds should be sown to a foot of row, the plants being thinned so that they will have 1½ to 2 inches of space for their development.

Spinach requires a very rich soil in order to make it grow quickly. A bed 5 feet wide and 30 feet in length and having about eight rows running the length of the bed will furnish enough spinach for the ordinary family. The entire spinach plant is removed by cutting just above the surface of the ground. Four ounces of seed is sufficient for a bed of 5 to 30 feet in size. Spinach is especially desirable as a part of the diet in the early spring.

CELERY

There is nothing particularly difficult about growing celery after the plants are started. The celery seed bed requires very careful watering until the plants are up and large enough to transplant. As a rule, it will be best for city gardeners to purchase plants that are ready for setting in the garden. Celery requires a rich soil and plenty of moisture.

Golden Plume and Easy Bleaching are among the best varieties for the home garden.

LETTUCE

No early garden would be complete without a bed of lettuce; however, only a small space is necessary to grow plenty for the average family. In the old-fashioned garden a small bed was spaded in one corner and the seed sown broadcast and raked into the soil just as soon as the ground was dry enough to work in the spring. As the plants grew and began to crowd one another they were thinned, and those that were pulled out were used on the table. Later, when the plants became larger, they were cut off just above the ground.

Lettuce requires very rich soil and plenty of moisture, will not withstand continued hot weather, and is one of the few crops that can be planted in back-yard gardens that are shaded a portion of the time. A 5-cent packet of seed will produce all the plants required for the small garden. A good method is to sow the seed in a box in the house and transplant the small plants to a bed or to rows in the garden. Lettuce is not injured by a light frost, especially if the plants have been grown in the open. The seed or plants may be planted between other crops that require a longer period for their development than lettuce. Two plantings should be made in the spring and one in the late summer, in order to have a supply for a considerable period.

Grand Rapids and Early Curled Simpson are the leading varieties of loose-leaf lettuce, while Big Boston, Iceberg, New York, Hansen, May King, and California Cream Butter are good heading sorts.

VEGETABLES THAT REQUIRE CONSIDERABLE SPACE IN THE GARDEN

There are a number of garden vegetables that require too much space for growing in the very small home garden. Among those included in this group are potatoes, sweetpotatoes, peas, sweet corn, squashes, muskmelons, and watermelons.

POTATOES

Potatoes are among the first crops that can be planted in the spring. They have no place in a small garden, but where space is available they should be included. A peck of seed potatoes, properly cut, will plant 300 feet of row and should yield 4 to 5 bushels. The usual method is to cut the seed two eyes to each piece, dividing the fleshy part of the potatoes as equally as possible. The seed should not be cut until the ground is all ready to receive it. Great care should be taken to get seed that is free from scab or other diseases.

Potatoes can be planted in the North just as soon as the frost is all out of the ground and the soil dry enough to work. In the South the planting date will be governed by the season and the time that the young plants will be safe from spring freezes. It generally takes three to five weeks after planting in the Southern States for the potatoes to come up. In the North they will appear in a shorter period if weather conditions are favorable.

PEAS

Peas, often called English peas, require considerable space. In order to be of real value, at least 15 feet of row should be planted for each person in the family. Peas are one of the first crops that can be planted in the spring. In the North this planting can be made just as soon as the ground can be worked, and two or even three plantings should be made in order to have a continuous supply. The later plantings rarely yield as well as the earlier ones. In the South peas are planted about the same time as early potatoes, or a little earlier.

Peas require a rather rich soil with a little fertilizer added, as they make a quick growth. First spade and rake the ground until it is fine and mellow, then open a furrow 2 to 3 inches deep with the corner of a hoe. Scatter the seeds broadcast in the furrow, or space them at the rate of 12 to 15 peas to a foot, and cover them. In heavy soils the seeds should not be covered so deeply as in light or sandy soils. If the ground is cold, the seeds may be 10 days or 2 weeks in coming up, and if there should be a heavy rain meantime the crust forming on the surface of the soil should be carefully broken over the rows with a steel rake.

Little Marvel, Alaska, Gradus, and Thomas Laxton are among the leading early sorts. The Champion of England and Telephone are considered good medium and late varieties.

The extra-early sorts may be planted with the rows as close as 24 inches apart where hand cultivation is practiced. The later and larger growing varieties require a space of about 3 feet between the rows. For securing the best yields the late maturing as well as the early maturing sorts should be planted early.

Several of the early varieties of peas can be grown without supports, but they do better if given something to climb on. The late varieties for the most part make a strong growth and require supports. Brush, where it may be had, woven-wire netting, a wire fence, or strings on stakes make satisfactory supports for peas. The supports should be in place when the peas come up, in order that the plants may climb them from the first. Early spring peas occupy the land a comparatively short time and may be followed by late cabbage, beets, turnips, kale, spinach, or some other crop. A planting of peas made late in the summer will often give a fall crop that is ready for use just before frost in the autumn.

SWEET CORN

Sweet corn requires so much space that it should be grown only in large gardens. The rows should be at least 3 feet apart and the individual plants 15 to 18 inches apart if in drills, and 2½ feet apart if in hills of three plants each for early varieties and 3 feet for late large sorts. Corn requires a rich soil and should not be planted until the ground has warmed considerably. A pint of seed will plant 400 to 500 feet of row in either drills or hills. Cover the seed 1½ to 2 inches deep and thin to three stalks in a hill or to single stalks 15 to 18 inches apart in drills.

Golden Bantam, Early Evergreen, and Howling Mob are leading early varieties. Country Gentleman and Stowell Evergreen are among the leading medium and late varieties. For a continuous supply, plant Golden Bantam as early as possible, then follow in a few days with Howling Mob. Two weeks later plant Country Gentleman or Stowell Evergreen and follow with additional plantings of some good late variety every three weeks until midsummer.

SWEETPOTATOES

For an early crop, sweetpotato plants are started in a hotbed, and they must not be set in the open until all danger of frost is past and the ground is well warmed up. They usually thrive best when planted on wide ridges some 3 to 4 feet apart and 12 to 15 inches apart in the row. Any good garden fertilizer will answer for this crop, and it is best applied either in small trenches or to the surface of the ground before the ridges are thrown up. Frequent shallow cultivation should be given until the vines begin to run.

The Porto Rico and Nancy Hall are recommended for moist-fleshed sorts and the Big-Stem Jersey, Goldskin, and Yellow Jersey where dry-fleshed sweetpotatoes are desired.

VINE GROUP

The vine group includes cucumbers, summer and winter squashes, muskmelons, and watermelons.

Practically all of the vine crops can be trained to a wire fence or trellis or on wire netting. By this method they can be planted along a fence or beside a building where there is good sunlight, and the vines can be trained up out of the way of other crops. In case cantaloupes or squashes are grown on a trellis, it will be necessary to support the fruits by means of bagging or cloth slings.

All of the vine crops require plenty of fertility in the soil. In addition to a shovelful of manure and a handful of fertilizer in each hill, a small quantity of commercial fertilizer may be worked into the soil around each hill after the vines begin to spread over the ground. The fertilizer should not be placed closer than a foot from the base of the plants and should be scattered over a considerable area. The space required by these crops precludes them from the small garden except where they are trained on wire or on a trellis, as already indicated. Beginners are advised to grow only summer squash and cucumber, if any.

CUCUMBERS

One or two hills will produce enough cucumbers for the average family. Each hill should be given about 50 square feet of space, or 7 feet in each direction. The hills should be made several days before planting, with a shovelful of manure mixed thoroughly with the soil of each hill. About a dozen seeds should be scattered in each hill and covered to a depth of about an inch. Later, the plants should be thinned to two or three in a hill.

Cucumbers are very susceptible to cold and should not be planted until all danger of frost is past. The plants may be started indoors by planting the seeds in pots, paper bands, or quart berry boxes filled with soil; then set in the garden when the weather is warm. The young cucumber plants are frequently destroyed by a small beetle. The easiest way to protect the plants is by covering the hills with fine wire netting.

Arlington White Spine is a common variety.

MUSKMELONS

Muskmelons, usually called cantaloupes, are grown in exactly the same way as cucumbers. The Netted Gem, Emerald Gem, Eden Gem, Burrell Gem, Early Hackensack, Hearts of Gold, Tiptop, Hoodoo, and Hale Best are among the leading varieties.

WATERMELONS

Watermelons require too much space for planting in a small garden. The cultivation of watermelons is practically the same as that of squashes. The Kleckley Sweets and Florida Favorite are among the best small watermelons for home growing.

SQUASHES

Two varieties of summer squashes are suited for growing in city gardens. These are the Summer Crookneck and Pattypan. The summer squashes are of bush habit of growth and do not require much space. Three to five hills of either of the kinds mentioned will supply the ordinary family. The hills should be 4 to 5 feet apart. Plant 8 or 10 seeds to a hill, covering them to a depth of an inch, and when the plants are well established thin them to three in a hill.

The Hubbard squash and Boston Marrow form true vines and require more space than the summer bush varieties. The fruits of the summer varieties are used while they are young and tender, but those of the fall and winter varieties are allowed to get fully ripe before being gathered and stored. Four or five hills will be sufficient, and a space of 10 to 12 feet should be allowed between the hills.

THE SMALL VEGETABLE GARDEN

SUGGESTIONS FOR UTILIZING LIMITED AREAS

FARMERS' BULLETIN 818
UNITED STATES DEPARTMENT OF AGRICULTURE

Prepared under the Direction of the Bureau of Plant Industry
WM. A. TAYLOR, Chief

Washington, D. C.   April, 1917

BY THE exercise of care and forethought in planning succession crops and rotations and by the utilization of every foot of available space it is possible to grow considerable quantities of vegetables on limited areas and so supplement the family food supply. The principal factors in accomplishing this are the use of seed boxes and hotbeds to give plants an early start in spring before seeds may be planted outdoors, the use of outside seed beds to carry plants for main-season crops while early crops are occupying the garden space, and the planting of late or succession crops as soon as earlier plants have been removed.

In order that gardening may be carried on successfully in such an intensive way it is especially important that soil of good texture be available, and that it be well supplied with humus and plant food. It is essential also, as in all gardening, that sufficient moisture be present, that the garden be kept free of weeds, and that the soil be cultivated frequently and well.

In the following pages specific suggestions are made for planning an intensive garden enterprise, for preparing the soil and maintaining its fertility, and for planting and growing the crops.

THE SMALL VEGETABLE GARDEN.

CONTENTS.

	Page.		Page.
Essentials of gardening	3	Gardener's planting table	18
Planning the small garden	4	Cultivation	24
Choosing crops	8	Irrigation	25
Aids to earliness (hotbed, seed box, cold frame)	9	Protecting plants from diseases and pests	25
Tools	12	Cultural suggestions for the commoner vegetables	28
Preparing the soil	14	Vegetables for winter use	42
Planting vegetables in the open	16	Fruits in the small garden	44

ESSENTIALS OF GARDENING.

THE primary needs for successful vegetable gardening on a small scale are the same as those for gardening on a large scale. On limited plots, however, greater emphasis must be placed on intensive culture and carefully arranged rotations so that every available foot of space may be made to produce the maximum yield.

The essentials of all gardening are soil of suitable texture containing available plant food, water to dissolve the plant food so that the plant rootlets may make use of it, seeds or plants which will produce the desired crops, sunshine and warmth to bring about germination and plant development, and cultivation. Much also depends upon the gardener and the care he bestows on his enterprise.

Other factors—location and exposure—can not always receive much consideration in gardening small plots since there is ordinarily little room for choice. Such spaces are located usually in yards, or the choice of location is restricted in other ways by the necessity that the spaces be accessible to dwellings. When a possibility for the exercise of choice does exist, however, several considerations should be kept in mind by the gardener. It should be recognized that frost is less likely to injure vegetables planted on high ground than those planted in low places or valleys into which the heavier cold air commonly settles; that crops will mature more rapidly on land that has a sunny, southern exposure than on other plots; that the garden should be fairly level, but well drained; and that a warm, sandy loam will produce an earlier crop than a heavier soil that retains more water and less heat.

The soil is the storehouse of plant food and should, therefore, have a relatively open texture so that the rootlets of vegetables may extend themselves readily in their search for sustenance. A high proportion of humus or rotted vegetable material is desirable in the soil, since it produces an open texture, adds nitrogen, insures the presence of beneficial bacteria, aids in unlocking plant food from mineral particles, and increases the moisture-retaining properties of the soil.

About 50 per cent of ordinary earth is not soil at all, but consists of air and water. Water makes the soluble plant food that is present in the soil freely available, while the air in the soil makes possible bacterial development and facilitates chemical action, which makes additional plant food available.

IMPORTANCE OF A GOOD SEED BED.

The cultivation of crops is important because the stirring and loosening of the soil directly conserves moisture to some extent, kills weeds, which draw moisture and plant food at the expense of the crops, and incorporates air into the soil.

Too much emphasis can not be laid on the preparation of a good seed bed. A seed bed of fine tilth—made such by deep plowing, careful harrowing, and fining of the soil—is the foundation of good gardening. It is essential for the proper germination of seeds and growth of young plants. The soil must be friable and free from clods. A clod locks up plant food and prevents its utilization by the plant. Good soil and fine tilth furnish best conditions for root development. Upon the fine, hairy, fibrous, feeding roots, which are possible only in well-tilled soil, the plant depends for its stockiness and growth.

The careful gardener will regard his whole garden as a seed bed and will cultivate and fertilize it accordingly.

FERTILIZERS.

Fertilizers, the plant foods for the garden, should be carefully selected. Nitrogen, which stimulates leaf growth, is best supplied by turning under rich, well-rotted, or composted manure or rotting vegetable matter. Sheep manure and poultry droppings will hurry plants along more rapidly than most chemical fertilizers. These substances, as well as bone meal, also a valuable fertilizer, usually may be obtained from seed stores.

PLANNING THE SMALL GARDEN.

With a little forethought a comparatively small tract of land may be made to supply the average family with fresh vegetables throughout the growing season. Most owners of small gardens are content to raise a single crop on each plot of land at their disposal. It is quite possible, however, to grow two or three crops of some vegetables in one season, and if these are properly selected the home-grown produce should be both better and cheaper than any that can be purchased on the market.

Just what vegetables are to be grown depends, of course, upon the individual tastes of the family. In general the aim of the home gardener should be to raise vegetables in which freshness is an important quality. Peas, string beans, Lima beans, asparagus, and sweet corn, for example, lose much if they are not cooked almost immediately after they are picked. On the other hand, as good

FIG. 1.—A back-yard vegetable garden which gives evidence of having received the care and attention that are essential to success in small-scale gardening.

potatoes usually can be bought as can be grown. Moreover, potatoes occupy a large area in proportion to their yield and consume in a back yard or small garden valuable space which, in most cases, could be put to much more profitable use. This may be true also, in some cases, of corn, cucumbers, squashes, and melons.

It will pay the home gardener to grow certain specialties of which he may be fond, and which may be troublesome or expensive to purchase. Okra is an example of this class, and little beds of parsley, chives, or other herbs take up very little room and provide the housewife with additions for her table, which are most welcome if they can be picked at the right moment without trouble.

THE GARDEN DIAGRAM.

If the small garden plot, however, is to be made to bring the maximum returns in economy and pleasure to the owner, every available foot of it must be made to work continuously. This can be accomplished only by careful planning, and it is recommended, therefore, that a complete lay-out for the garden be drawn up in advance. A typical plan of this character is shown in figure 1. This plan, of course, will be of use chiefly as an example, and in most cases a different arrangement will be necessary to meet the conditions surrounding individual garden spaces. On the plan the gardener may indicate the approximate date when each of his projected crops is to be planted. No more space should be allotted to each than is needed to furnish a sufficient quantity of the vegetable for family consumption or for other known needs. In many cases, also, space should be left between the rows for the interplanting of later crops and for easy cultivation. Plants which make a high growth and cause heavy shade should not be located where they will interfere with sun-loving small plants. It is well also to separate perennials, such as rhubarb and asparagus, which are not cultivated, from plants which must be tilled.

THE DIAGRAM AS A RECORD.

If a garden is planned in this way and the scheme carried out, the plan should be kept for use the following year, with notes of the success or failure of the different items in it. For example, if too much or too little of any vegetable was grown, this fact should be recorded. It is not desirable, however, to follow too closely the same plan in succeeding years. The same kind of vegetables should not be grown twice, if this can be avoided, in the same part of the garden. The danger of attack by diseases and insects is heightened when vegetables of the same kind follow each other repeatedly in a given space, such as a row or bed. If a radically different kind of plant is grown in a space, on the other hand, disease spores and insects, though present in the soil, probably will not attack the second crop.

In making a diagram of the garden it is well to use a tough paper, such as heavy wrapping paper, which will stand repeated handling and use out of doors. A fairly large scale should be adopted, so that full notes can be kept in the spaces representing rows. If the garden is fairly large or abnormally long, the diagram may be made in separate sections for the sake of convenience.

A BACK-YARD GARDEN.

The garden shown in the diagram (fig. 2) was a city back yard 25 by 70 feet in dimensions near New York City. It happened

THE SMALL VEGETABLE GARDEN.

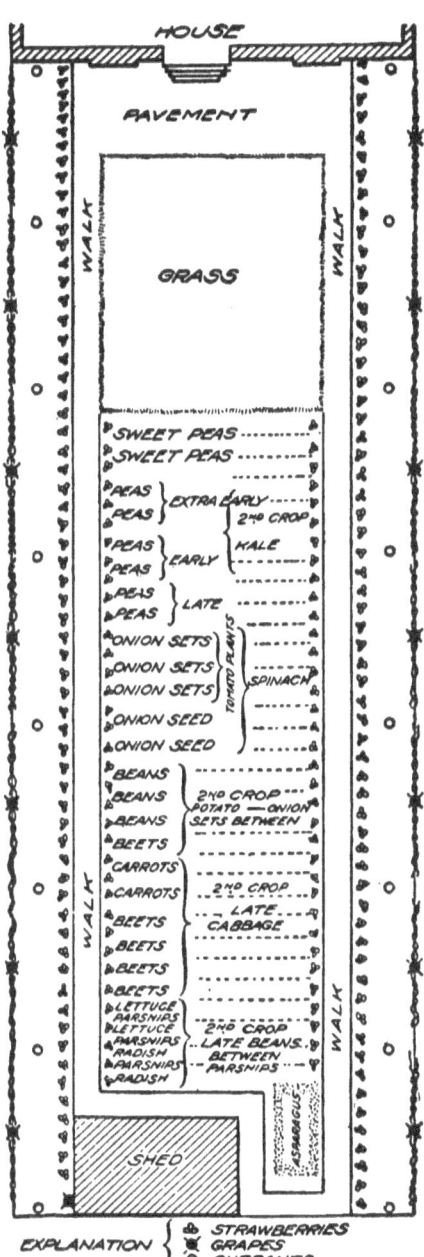

Fig. 2.—A typical back-yard garden plan, showing a possible arrangement for permanent and annual plants.

to be bounded on two sides by a board fence, and advantage was taken of this fact to plant and train grape vines. Strawberry plants were set alongside the flagstone walks and currant bushes between the walks and the fence. In the space between the bushes and the strawberries low-growing vegetables, such as bush beans, peppers, eggplants, and the like, were set out. In a space about 12 feet wide between the walks low-growing, quick-maturing varieties of early vegetables were planted in such a way that later-maturing varieties could be put out at proper intervals between them. The early plantings consisted of radishes, early beets, lettuce, carrots, and a few parsnips. The beets gave way later to a few late cabbage plants. The sunniest portion of the yard was turned over to tomatoes, of which there were about a dozen plants trained to a single stem and set about 18 inches apart in each direction. Early and late peas were put out in the least sunny portions of the yard. Later, in the fall, spinach, kale, and potato-onion sets were planted in order to provide a supply of green succulents for the winter and early spring.

IMPORTANCE OF SUNLIGHT.

In making the garden plan the gardener should recognize that no amount of fertilizer, watering, and cultivation will make up for the absence of sunlight in a garden. Careful consideration should be given to how many hours a day any part of the yard is in shadow from buildings, fences, or trees. If a successful garden is to be maintained, the greater portion of the plot must have at least five hours of sunlight a day. As a rule foliage crops, such as lettuce, spinach, and kale, do fairly well in partial shade, but even these need sunshine two or three hours a day. Plants which must ripen fruits, such as tomatoes and eggplant, should have the sunniest locations.

CHOOSING CROPS.

Vegetable seed should be ordered in advance of the time for planting in the open, so that they will be on hand for planting in flats or frames and also for use outdoors as soon as the weather and the condition of the soil make planting possible. Before ordering seed it is a good idea to look over the garden plot, decide on the best location for each vegetable, and determine how much seed will be required for the space available for each variety. The garden plan may then be drawn.

SEED FOR A FAMILY OF FOUR.

The following are the approximate quantities of seed that should be purchased for a garden which is to supply vegetables for successive plantings throughout the season for a family of four:

Beans, snap	1 pint.	Parsnips	½ ounce.
Beans, pole Lima	½ pint.	Salsify	1 ounce.
Beans, bush Lima	½ pint.	Squash, summer	½ ounce.
Cabbage, early	½ ounce.	Squash, Hubbard type	½ ounce.
Carrot	1 ounce.	Cauliflower	1 packet.
Celery	1 ounce.	Eggplant	1 packet.
Cucumber	½ ounce.	Parsley	1 packet.
Kale, or Swiss chard	½ ounce.		

For most of the vegetables listed the plantings may consist of the entire quantities mentioned. Relatively small quantities of cauliflower, eggplant, and parsley will be sufficient for most families, however.

The following vegetables undoubtedly will be planted in larger amounts than those just mentioned, and the amounts of seed given will be a guide for ordinary requirements. Some families may need more of the various vegetables and others less:

Beet	2 ounces.	Radish	1 ounce.
Cabbage, late	½ ounce.	Spinach	½ pound in spring and ½ pound in fall
Corn, sweet	1 pint.		
Lettuce	½ ounce.		
Muskmelon	1 ounce.	Tomatoes, late	¼ ounce.
Onion sets	2 quarts.	Turnips	1 ounce.
Peas, garden	2 to 4 quarts.		

The entire supply of seeds of string bean, bush Lima bean, sweet corn, lettuce, peas, and radish should not be planted at one time, but successive plantings two to three weeks apart should be made so that a fresh supply of the vegetables may be had throughout the season.

Of early Irish potatoes 1 peck to ½ bushel will be required, and of late potatoes ½ bushel to 1 bushel, or more, depending upon the amount of ground available for this purpose. If abundant space is available, it may be well to grow enough Irish potatoes to last throughout the winter.

If the family wishes to raise vegetables to supply current needs and also to supply a surplus for canning, the amounts indicated above should be increased considerably.[1]

FIG. 3.—A hill of beans started in a berry box in the house long before the seeds may be planted in the open garden.

AIDS TO EARLINESS.

The hotbed, the "flat" or seed box, and the cold frame are the gardener's greatest aids in raising early crops. The hotbed and the flat enable him to plant seed and produce seedlings long before most of the seeds may be planted out of doors and before those which have been planted in the plot have begun to germinate. The cold frame enables him to get the seedlings produced in the hotbed gradually accustomed to outdoor conditions and to raise these into strong, sturdy planting stock by the time the garden is ready for them. Resetting from a hotbed into a cold frame, or from one flat into another, or into pots, gives most plants a better root system and makes them stockier and more valuable for transplanting into the open ground. Besides being used in hardening plants that have been

---

[1] The home gardener should find useful Farmers' Bulletins 359, Canning Vegetables in the Home; 521, Canning Tomatoes, Home and Club Work; 255, Home Vegetable Garden; and 647, Home Garden in the South. The latter is designed particularly for use in the warmer climates, but contains many suggestions that can be adapted readily by home gardeners in the North. The Department of Agriculture will supply these bulletins free on application as long as its stock for free distribution lasts.

started in the hotbed, the cold frame is utilized in mild climates instead of a hotbed for starting plants before seeds can be planted safely in the open. In the extreme South the cold frame is much more extensively used than the hotbed, but each has its place in garden economy.

Still another method of giving plants an early start is used extensively for beans, cucumbers, melons, sweet corn, and other warmth-loving plants. This consists in planting enough seeds for a "hill" in berry boxes filled with soil. (Fig. 3.) The boxes are kept in the house or in greenhouses until the garden soil becomes warm, by which time the plants should have reached a considerable degree of development. The bottoms of the boxes are then cut away and the remaining frame is sunk with the plants in their permanent location in the garden.

STARTING EARLY VEGETABLES IN THE HOUSE.

The flat or seed box (fig. 4) which is kept in the house is perhaps the most practical device for use by the home gardener for starting early vegetables. By its use earlier crops of tomatoes, cabbage, cauliflower, Brussels sprouts, peppers, eggplant, and lettuce can be had with little outlay for equipment. Early potatoes sometimes are forced in the same way. Seeds

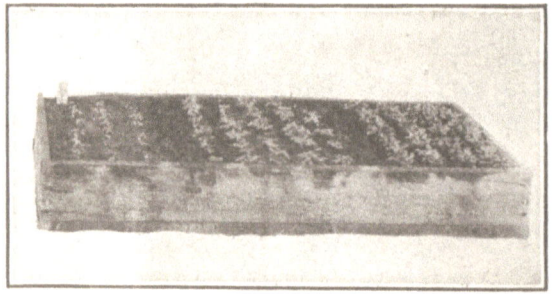

FIG. 4.—Flat or seed box for use in starting plants in the house.

so planted germinate and are ready for transplanting by the time it is safe to sow the same kind of seed in the open ground. When danger of frost is over and the soil is dry enough to work, therefore, the early garden may be started with seedlings well above the surface. Transplanting, if properly done, instead of injuring seems to help such plants to develop a strong root system.

HOW TO MAKE AND USE A SEED BOX.

Any sort of wooden box filled with good soil answers the purpose, but the following specific suggestions for a box of convenient size may be useful. Construct a box 3 to 4 inches deep, 12 to 14 inches wide, and 20 to 24 inches long. A layer of about 1 inch of gravel or cinders should be placed in the bottom of the box. It should then be filled nearly full with rich garden soil or soil enriched with decayed leaves or manure. The rich soil beneath the family woodpile or around decaying logs is splendid for this purpose. The soil should be pressed down firmly with a small piece of board and rows made one-fourth to one-half inch deep and 2 inches apart crosswise of the box. The seed should be distributed 8 or 10 to the inch in the rows and be covered. The soil should be watered and the box set in a warm place in the light. The best location is just inside a sunny window. Water enough must be given from time to time to cause the seeds to germinate and grow thriftily, but not enough to leak through the box. If a piece of glass is used to cover the box, it will hold the moisture in the soil and hasten the germination of the seeds.

When the plants are from an inch to an inch and a half high they should be thinned to 1 or 2 inches apart in the row, so as to give them space enough to make a strong stocky growth. If it is desired to keep the plants which are thinned out, they may be set 2 inches apart each way in boxes similar to the seed box. When the weather becomes mild the box of plants should be set out of doors part of the time so that the plants will "harden off" in preparation for transplanting to the garden later. A good watering should be given just before the plants are taken out of the box for transplanting, so that a large ball of earth will stick to the roots of each one.

THE HOTBED.

Locate the hotbed in some sheltered but not shaded spot which has a southern exposure. The most convenient size is a box-like structure 6 feet wide and any multiple of 3 feet long, so that standard 3 by 6 foot hotbed sash may be used. The frame should be 12 inches high in the back and 8 inches in the front. This slope is for the purpose of securing a better angle for the sun's rays and should be faced toward the south.

The hotbed not only must collect any heat it can from the sun, but also must generate heat of its own from fermentation in fresh manure. Fresh horse manure, free from stable litter, is best for generating heat.

If the hotbed is to be an annual affair, make an excavation 18 inches to 2 feet deep, about 2 feet greater in length and width than the frame carrying the sash. Line the excavation with plank or with a brick or concrete wall. A drain to carry off surplus water is essential. This may consist of either tile or pipe extending to a low portion of the garden or a trench partially filled with coarse stones covered with a layer of hay or sod and then filled level with soil.

After a sufficient amount of fresh horse manure has been accumulated fill the hotbed pit, and while it is being filled tramp the manure as firmly and as evenly as possible. When the ground level is reached, place the frame in position and bank the sides and ends with manure. Place about 3 inches of good garden loam on top of the manure inside the frame and cover it with the sash. After the heat has reached its maximum and has subsided to between 80° and 90° F. it will be safe to plant the seeds. Select the plumpest, freshest seeds obtainable. Use standard varieties, and get them from reliable seed houses.

Keep the bed partially dark until the seeds germinate.

Fig. 5.—Cold frame open for ventilating plants.

After germination, however, the plants will need all the light possible, exclusive of the direct rays of the sun, to keep them growing rapidly. This is a crisis in plant life, and ventilating and watering with great care are of prime importance. Too close planting and too much heat and water cause the plants to become spindling. Water the plants on clear days, in the morning, and ventilate immediately to dry the foliage and to prevent mildew.

THE COLD FRAME.

The cold frame (fig. 5), so useful in hardening plants started in the hotbed and for starting plants in mild climates, is constructed in much the same way as the hotbed, except that no manure is used, and the frame may be covered either with glass sash or with canvas. A cold frame may be built on the surface of the ground, but a more permanent structure suitable for holding plants over winter will require a pit 18 to 24 inches deep. The cold frame should be filled with a good potting soil. The plants should have more ventilation in the cold frame, but should not receive so much water. It is best to keep the soil rather dry.

In transplanting, remember that plants usually thrive better if transplanted into ground that has been freshly cultivated. Transplanting to the open field is best done in cool, cloudy weather and in the afternoon. This prevents the sun's rays from causing the plant to lose too much moisture through evaporation. In transplanting the gardener will find a child's express wagon an excellent trolley tray for bedding out his seedlings.

TOOLS.

The necessary tools for preparing and caring for the small garden are few. A spade or garden fork for digging, a hoe, a steel-tooth rake, a trowel, and a dibble or pointed stick complete the list of essentials. The gardener will find it convenient, however, to possess some additional implements. (Fig. 6.) If tree roots underlie any portion of the garden plot and must be cut away, a hatchet, ax, or mattock will be a real necessity. If the soil of the plot has become compacted, as where walks have existed, a pick may be needed for digging. Perhaps in such cases it will be most economical to fill both cutting and digging needs by purchasing a pick-ax which has a pick point at one end of the head and a cutting blade at the other. Apparatus for watering plants also should be included. This may be a watering pot of generous proportions or, where running water is available, a

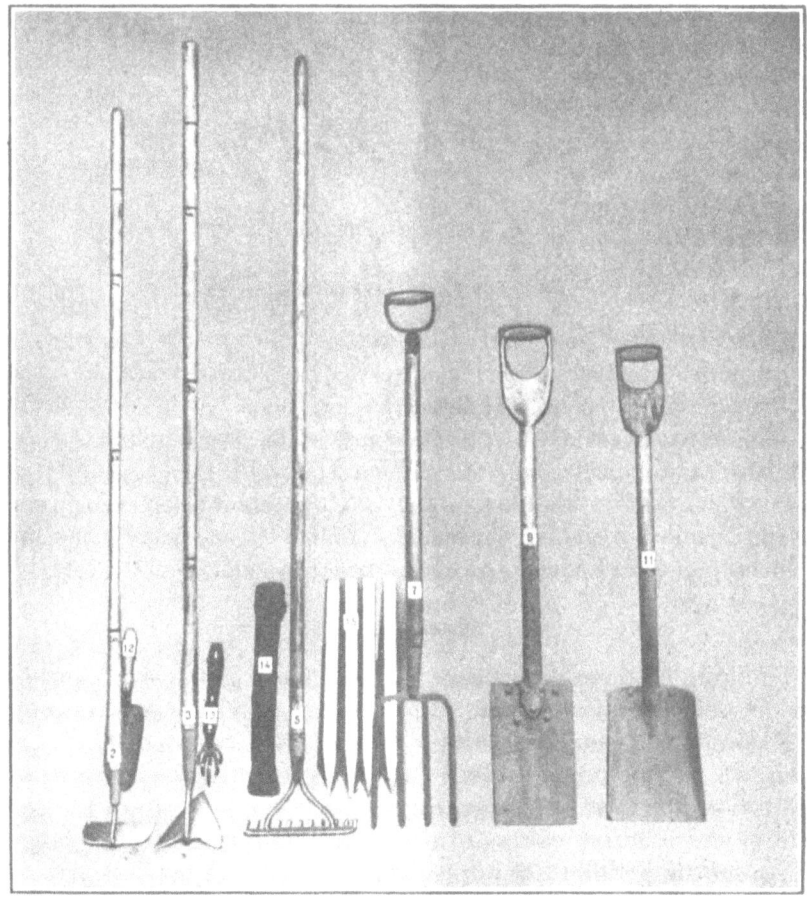

FIG. 6.—A set of garden tools, including the essential implements and a few others. (2) Hoe, (3) heart-shaped furrow hoe, (5) steel-tooth rake, (7) fork, (9) spade, (11) shovel, (12) trowel, (13) scratch weeder, (14) line, (15) stakes. Note that the handles of some of the longer implements are marked off in feet and half feet for convenience in measuring.

hose. In order that rows may be made straight and uniform a substantial line or cord should be provided.

A most convenient implement for use in the home garden, especially where the plot is fairly large, is a hand cultivator or wheel hoe. (Fig. 7.) This implement is a miniature cultivator or plow, with adjustable blades, mounted on a wheel or wheels, and is pushed along by hand. Attachments make possible either the turning of small furrows, the stirring of the soil, or the removal of weeds. Much time and labor may be saved by such a device.

Among the other implements which may be useful in the home garden but which are not essential are planting and cultivating hoes of special shapes, a combination hoe and rake, a wheelbarrow, a shovel, hand weeding tools, and other small implements for special uses (fig. 8).

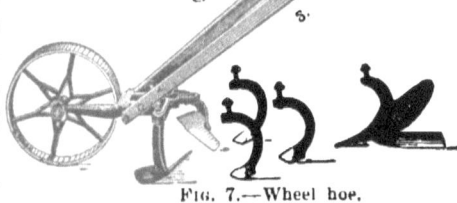
Fig. 7.—Wheel hoe.

PREPARING THE SOIL.

A simple test to determine when garden soil is ready for plowing or working is to take a handful of earth from the surface and close the fingers tightly on it. If the earth compacted in this way is dry enough for cultivation, it will fall apart when the hand is opened. This test is applicable only to comparatively heavy soils, but it is these which receive the most injury if they are worked when wet. On such soils overzealous gardeners not only waste their time but frequently do actual damage by attempting to work them too early.

BREAKING.

The kind of preparation that must be given to the small garden and the amount of work that will be required will depend largely, of course, on the condition of the plot and the use to which it has been put. If the ground selected for the garden has been firmed by much tramping, as is often the case in back yards, it can not be got into proper condition without the expenditure of considerable labor. When plowing with a team can be practiced that is the best method for giving the ground its initial breaking. The surface, of course, should be harrowed as soon as possible after plowing.

If the plot can not be plowed, the gardener must resort to the use of a garden fork or spade or, in the case of very hard spots, a mattock. The soil should be well loosened to the depth of the spade or fork. If heavy clay is encountered at this depth, it should not be turned up to the surface, but the slices of soil should be kept in their normal position. As soon as each spade or fork full of earth is loosened, it should be broken up by blows with the back of the implement. Later the freshly dug surface should be fined and smoothed with a steel-tooth rake. It is not sufficient that the surface be made fine; the soil should be well pulverized to the depth of the digging. Any sod or plant growth on the garden plot should be turned under to rot and form humus. In turning under sod with a spade or fork it is well to reverse each segment so that foliage will be down and roots up.

The first digging of a plot of ground which has not before been cultivated is likely to be a laborious task, and may even take away the enthusiasm of the would-be gardener. After this portion of the work is done, however, the fining of the soil, planting, and cultivation are not arduous. It may be well in many cases for the gardener to employ some one to break his ground, whether this be done with plow, spade, or fork.

FIG. 8.—Small hand tools for the garden. From left to right they are: Hand weeder, dibble, onion hoe, trowel, and scratch or claw weeder.

IMPROVING SOIL TEXTURE.

It is desirable that the soil of the garden be as open and light as possible. Where a natural loam exists in the plot good texture can be given by digging and cultivating. Where the soil is heavy, containing much clay, however, other steps are necessary. If clean sand is available this may be mixed with the soil. Well-sifted coal ashes which, unlike wood ashes, have no fertilizing value, are useful in lightening the soil. Care should be taken that no coarse cinders or pieces of partly burned coal are added to the soil with the ashes.

Lime added to the soil also will tend to lighten it and will, at the same time, correct acidity. A thin coat of air-slaked lime should be spread on the ground and worked in well. Lime is not a plant food, but its function in gardening is important none the less. By correcting acidity it makes possible the development of countless soil bacteria which aid in unlocking plant food from the mineral particles of the soil and in making these substances available for the plants. In acid soils these helpful organisms do not thrive, and in their absence vegetables do not grow at their best.

FERTILIZERS.

After the soil has been got into good mechanical condition, it usually is desirable to apply some form of fertilizer. Barnyard or stable manure, which furnishes both plant food and humus, undoubtedly is the best, and applications of from 20 to 30 tons to the acre are satisfactory. This is roughly equivalent to from 400 to 600 pounds, or several wheelbarrow loads, for each plot 20 by 20 feet. The manure should be distributed evenly over the surface, and later worked in with a hoe and rake.

Frequently it is advisable also to apply commercial fertilizer. An application of 1,000 to 1,500 pounds to the acre, or 10 to 15 pounds per plot 20 feet square, usually is sufficient. In order to supply potash, if this is needed, unleached wood ashes may be distributed over the garden at the rate of 1,000 pounds to the acre, or 10 pounds to each plot 20 feet square. Wet or leached ashes have less fertilizer value. Double the quantity of these should be used. In order to start the plants in the spring, applications of 100 pounds to the acre of nitrate of soda, or 1 pound to each 20-foot square, may be used. By far the best way to use nitrate of soda in the small garden, however, is to dissolve a teaspoonful of the chemical in a gallon of water and use the solution for watering young plants. It is important to remember that no form of commercial fertilizer will yield good results unless the soil is well supplied with humus.

Reference already has been made to the use of prepared sheep manure as a fertilizer. When this plant food can be obtained at a reasonable price, it is perhaps the safest concentrated fertilizer for use by the home gardener. It will not pay to broadcast prepared sheep manure. Small quantities should be applied under the drill when the seeds are planted or the plants set out. Later applications may be worked in with a trowel around the plants.

PLANTING VEGETABLES IN THE OPEN.

WHEN TO PLANT.

Vegetables may be divided into two classes—" cold temperature " and " warm temperature " vegetables. When peach and plum trees are in blossom, or, where these trees do not occur, when silver maples put forth leaves, or catkins appear on willows and poplars, it is time to sow in the open ground the seeds of lettuce, spinach, kale, endive, radish, parsley, beets, turnips, cabbage, cauliflower, Brussels sprouts, carrots, round-seeded peas, and onions. The wrinkled peas should not be planted until later, as they are more likely to rot in cool ground than are the smooth varieties. When the apple trees bloom, or when the dogwood and white oak buds unfold, it is time to plant the heat-loving vegetables such as cucumbers, beans, sweet corn, okra, pumpkin, and squash. This is an old approximation for planting dates, but has been found in most cases to be satisfactory.

Planting times may be fixed in still another way on the basis of the occurrence of frost. Frost ordinarily will kill tender growths of vegetables, but young plants of a few kinds will survive light frosts. Among the latter, which may be called Group I, are cabbage, lettuce, Irish potatoes, early peas (smooth seeded), onion seeds and sets, parsnips, salsify, beets, radishes, and such salad plants as kale, spinach, and mustard.

A "second early" group of vegetables, which may be called Group II, may be planted as soon as danger of frost is over. In this group are included lettuce plants and seeds, radishes, wrinkled peas, carrots, and early sweet corn.

A week or 10 days after the seeds and plants of Group II are placed in the ground, string beans and late sweet corn, constituting Group III, may be planted.

A group of plants, which may be called Group IV, should be planted only after the ground has begun to warm up. In this group are cucumbers, melons, squashes, pumpkins, Lima beans, and tomato, eggplant, and pepper plants.

Detailed suggestions for planting are given in a table on pages 18 and 19

DEPTHS OF PLANTING.

No general rule can be given with regard to the depth for planting seeds, since different varieties of vegetables and different soils necessitate different practices. The smaller the seeds, usually, the shallower the planting should be. In heavy clay or moist soils the covering should be lighter than in sandy or dry soils.

GARDENER'S PLANTING TABLE.

Quantity of seeds or number of plants required for a row 100 feet in length, with distances to plant, times for planting, and period required for production of crop.

[Brackets indicate that a late or second crop may be planted the same season.]

Kind of vegetable.	Seeds or plants required for 100 feet of row.	Distance for plants to stand—			Depth of planting.	Time of planting in open ground.		Ready for use after planting.
		Rows apart.		Plants apart in rows.		South.	North.	
		Horse cultivation.	Hand cultivation.					
Artichoke, globe	½ ounce	3 to 4 ft	2 to 3 ft	2 to 3 ft	1 to 2 in	Spring	Spring	15 months.
Artichoke, Jerusalem	2 qts. tubers	3 to 4 ft	1 to 2 ft	1 to 2 ft	2 to 3 in	Spring	Spring	6 to 8 months.
Asparagus, seed	1 ounce	30 to 36 in	1 to 2 ft	3 to 5 in	1 to 2 in	Autumn or early spring	Early spring	3 to 4 years.
Asparagus, plants	60 to 80 plants	3 to 5 ft	12 to 24 in	15 to 20 in	3 to 5 in	Autumn or early spring	Early spring	1 to 3 years.
Beans, bush	1 pint	30 to 36 in	18 to 24 in	5 or 8 to ft	½ to 2 in	February to April. [August to September.]	April to July	40 to 65 day.
Beans, pole	½ pint	3 to 4 ft	3 to 4 ft	3 to 4 ft	1 to 2 in	Late spring	May and June	50 to 80 days.
Beets	2 ounces	24 to 36 in	12 to 18 in	5 or 6 to ft	1 to 2 in	February to April. [August to September.]	April to August	60 to 80 days.
Brussels sprouts	¼ ounce	30 to 36 in	24 to 30 in	16 to 24 in	½ in	January to July	May and June	90 to 120 days.
Cabbage, early	¼ ounce	30 to 36 in	24 to 30 in	12 to 18 in	½ in	October to December	March and April. (Start in hotbed during February.)	90 to 130 days
Cabbage, late	¼ ounce	30 to 40 in	24 to 36 in	16 to 24 in	½ in	June and July	May and June	90 to 130 days
Cardoon	½ ounce	3 ft	2 ft	12 to 18 in	1 to 2 in	Early spring	April and May	5 to 6 months.
Carrot	1 ounce	30 to 36 in	18 to 24 in	6 or 7 to ft	½ in	March and April. [September.]	April to June	75 to 110 days.
Cauliflower	¼ ounce	30 to 36 in	24 to 30 in	14 to 18 in	½ in	January and February. [June.]	April to June. (Start in hotbed during February or March.)	100 to 130 days.
Celeriac	¼ ounce	30 to 36 in	18 to 24 in	4 or 5 to ft	⅛ in	Late spring	May and June. (Start in cold frame during April.)	100 to 150 days.
Celery	¼ ounce	3 to 6 ft	18 to 36 in	4 to 8 in	⅛ in	August to October	May and June. (Start in hotbed or cold frame during March or April.)	120 to 150 days.
Chervil	1 ounce	30 to 36 in	18 to 24 in	3 or 4 to ft	1 in	Autumn	Autumn	1 year.
Chicory	¼ ounce	30 to 36 in	18 to 24 in	4 or 5 to ft	¼ in	March and April	May and June	5 to 6 months.
Citron	1 ounce	8 to 10 ft	8 to 10 ft	8 to 10 ft	1 to 2 in	March and April	May and June	100 to 130 days.
Collards	¼ ounce	30 to 36 in	24 to 30 in	14 to 18 in	½ in	May and June	Late spring	100 to 120 days.
Corn salad	2 ounces	30 in	12 to 18 in	5 or 6 to ft	½ to 1 in	January and February. [September and October.]	March to September	60 days.
Corn, sweet	¼ pint	36 to 42 in	30 to 36 in	30 to 36 in	1 to 2 in	February to April	May to July	60 to 100 days.
Cress, upland	½ ounce	30 in	12 to 18 in	4 or 5 to ft	½ to 1 in	January and February. [Autumn.]	March to May. [September]	30 to 40 days.

Cress, water	½ ounce	Broadcast			On surface	Early spring	April to September	60 to 70 days.
Cucumber	½ ounce	4 to 6 ft	4 to 6 ft	4 to 6 ft	1 to 2 in	February and March. [September.]	April to July	60 to 80 days.
Dandelion	½ ounce	30 in	18 to 24 in	8 to 12 in	⅛ in	Early spring or autumn	Early spring	6 to 12 months.
Eggplant	½ ounce	30 to 36 in	24 to 30 in	18 to 24 in	½ to 1 in	February to April	April and May. (Start in hotbed during March.)	100 to 140 days.
Endive	1 ounce	30 in	18 in	8 to 12 in	½ to 1 in	February to April	April. [July]	90 to 180 days.
Horse-radish	70 roots	30 to 40 in	24 to 30 in	14 to 20 in	3 to 4 in	Early spring	Early spring	1 to 2 years.
Kale, or borecole	¼ ounce	30 to 36 in	18 to 24 in	18 to 24 in	½ in	October to February	August and September. [March and April.]	90 to 120 days.
Kohl-rabi	½ ounce	30 to 36 in	18 to 24 in	4 to 8 in	½ in	September to March	March to May	60 to 80 days.
Leek	½ ounce	30 to 36 in	14 to 20 in	4 to 8 in	1 in	May to September	March to May	120 to 180 days.
Lettuce	½ ounce	30 in	12 to 18 in	4 to 6 in	½ in	September to March	March to September	60 to 90 days.
Melon, muskmelon	½ ounce	6 to 8 ft	6 to 8 ft	Hills 6 ft	1 to 2 in	February to April	April to June. (Start early plants in hotbed during March.)	120 to 150 days.
Melon, watermelon	1 ounce	8 to 12 ft	8 to 12 ft	Hills 10 ft	1 to 2 in	March to May	May and June	100 to 120 days.
Mustard	¼ ounce	30 to 36 in	12 to 18 in	4 or 5 to ft	¼ in	Autumn or early spring	March to May. [September]	60 to 90 days.
New Zealand spinach	1 ounce	36 in	24 to 36 in	12 to 18 in	1 to 2 in	Early spring	Early spring	60 to 100 days.
Okra, or gumbo	2 ounces	4 to 5 ft	3 to 4 ft	24 to 30 in	1 to 2 in	February to April	May and June	90 to 140 days.
Onion, seed	1 ounce	24 to 36 in	12 to 18 in	4 or 5 to ft	½ to 1 in	October to March	April and May	130 to 150 days.
Onion, sets	1 quart of sets	24 to 36 in	12 to 18 in	4 or 5 to ft	1 to 2 in	Early spring	Autumn and February to May.	90 to 120 days.
Parsley	¼ ounce	24 to 36 in	12 to 18 in	3 to 6 in	⅛ in	September to May	September and early spring	90 to 120 days.
Parsnip	½ ounce	30 to 36 in	18 to 24 in	5 or 6 to ft	½ to 1 in		April and May	125 to 160 days.
Peas	1 to 2 pints	3 to 4 ft	30 to 36 in	15 to ft	2 to 3 in	September to April	March to June	40 to 80 days.
Pepper	⅛ ounce	30 to 36 in	18 to 24 in	15 to 18 in	½ in	Early spring	May and June. (Start early plants in hotbed during March.)	100 to 140 days.
Physalis	½ ounce	30 to 36 in	18 to 24 in	18 to 24 in	½ in	March to May	May and June	130 to 160 days.
Potato, Irish	5 lbs. (or 9 bu. per acre).	30 to 36 in	24 to 36 in	14 to 18 in	4 in	January to April	March to June	80 to 140 days.
Potato, sweet	3 lbs. (or 75 slips).	3 to 5 ft	3 to 5 ft	14 in	3 in	April and May	May and June. (Start plants in hotbed during April.)	140 to 160 days.
Pumpkin	½ ounce	8 to 12 ft	8 to 12 ft	Hills 8 to 12 ft.	1 to 2 in	April and May	May to July	100 to 140 days.
Radish	1 ounce	24 to 36 in	12 to 18 in	8 to 12 to ft	½ to 1 in	September to April	March to September	20 to 40 days.
Rhubarb, seed	½ ounce	36 in	30 to 36 in	6 to 8 in	½ to 1 in		Early spring	2 to 4 years.
Rhubarb, plants	33 plants	3 to 5 ft	3 to 5 ft	3 ft	2 to 3 in		Autumn or early spring	1 to 3 years.
Rutabaga	¼ ounce	30 to 36 in	18 to 24 in	6 to 8 in	½ to 1 in	August and September	May and June	60 to 80 days.
Salsify	1 ounce	30 to 36 in	18 to 24 in	2 to 4 in	½ to 1 in		Early spring	120 to 180 days.
Spinach	1 ounce	30 to 36 in	12 to 18 in	7 or 8 to ft	1 to 2 in	September to February	September or very early spring.	30 to 60 days.
Squash, bush	½ ounce	3 to 4 ft	3 to 4 ft	Hills 3 to 4 ft.	1 to 2 in	Spring	April to June	60 to 80 days.
Squash, late	½ ounce	7 to 10 ft	7 to 10 ft	Hills 7 to 9 ft.	1 to 2 in	Spring	April to June	120 to 160 days.
Tomato	⅛ ounce	3 to 5 ft	3 to 4 ft	3 ft	½ to 1 in	December to March	May and June. (Start early plants in hotbed during February and March.)	100 to 140 days.
Turnip	½ ounce	24 to 36 in	18 to 24 in	6 or 7 to ft	¼ to ½ in	August to October	April. [July]	60 to 80 days.
Vegetable marrow	½ ounce	8 to 12 ft	8 to 12 ft	Hills 8 to 9 ft.	1 to 2 in	Spring	April to June	110 to 140 days.

SEED BEDS.

The gardener may find it desirable to reserve a small area of his garden for a seed bed in which some of the second crops for his rotations may be grown while the ground in which they are to develop is still occupied. In this way also advantage is taken of the fact that transplanting makes for stockiness. In seed-bed culture much the same practices are in force as in growing plantlets in flats and frames. The rows of seeds, however, are not spaced so closely in the outdoor seed beds as in the boxes and frames. When the plantlets crowd they may be thinned out or transplanted to another part of the seed bed. Late cabbage, lettuce, Brussels sprouts, cauliflower, etc., are plants that in many cases may be treated conveniently in this way.

FIG. 9.—Use of a rake handle and line in opening a furrow for planting.

PLANTING PRACTICES.

In planting many kinds of seeds in the garden thick sowings are made to insure a good stand, and the superfluous plants later are pulled up. Straight rows or drills should be used in all cases. The use of a line will make accuracy possible. The line is stretched between stakes at the ends of the row, and with this as a guide the furrow is then opened. This may be done with the end of a hoe or rake handle (fig. 9), with the corner of a hoe, or the point of a special furrow hoe, with a hand plow, or with the edge of a board pressed into the loosened soil. Small seeds may be shaken out of the packet by hand in a thin stream while the packet is held close to the bottom of the furrow. Larger seeds, like peas and beans, may be dropped from the hand. Mechanical planters, built like wheel hoes, may be purchased if the size of the garden justifies their use.

DRILLS, ROWS, AND HILLS.

Small plants which are to be left almost touching each other, as is the case with onions and carrots, are said to be grown in drills. Plants grown at fixed distances, as cabbages or potatoes, are in rows. When plants are grown at distances of several feet apart in both directions they are said to be in hills. Furrows are opened for planting in both drills and rows. Hills, however, may be opened with a spade or trowel. An excellent method of using fertilizer is to apply it in the drills, rows, or hills before planting. In such cases the fertilizer should be mixed carefully with the soil in the bottom of the opening before the seeds are deposited.

FINAL PLANTING TOUCHES.

In planting the gardener should keep in mind that to germinate and develop properly into sturdy plants the seed must be firmly imbedded in well-fined, moist soil. The condition of the soil beneath the seeds is most important, since it is in this soil that the rootlets on emerging must find sustenance. Air spaces or cracks may cause the rootlets to shrivel. It is well, therefore, especially if the soil is at all dry, to force the seeds gently into the soil, compacting it slightly. This may be done with the back of a hoe in the case of small seeds, or with the ball of the foot when large seeds such as beans and peas are being planted. The seeds should then be covered immediately with soil. This should be very slightly compacted over the seeds with the back of the hoe. If weather conditions are such that there is a tendency for the soil to bake over the drills and rows before the plants appear, it is well to rake very lightly with a steel-tooth rake. It may be necessary, also, to work the ground at the sides of the rows as the plants are breaking through the surface. This should be done very carefully to avoid injury to the tender shoots.

SETTING OUT PLANTS.

Plants grown in flats, hotbeds, or cold frames should be "hardened off" as has already been suggested, before they are to be planted out of doors. Another preliminary step, if the plants are too tall or succulent, is to trim away about one-half of the large leaves. Several hours before transplanting the plants should be watered thoroughly, so that the soil will be moist enough to stick to the roots in balls of considerable bulk. After staking out rows and marking planting positions, lift the plants out with a trowel, keeping as much soil as possible on the roots. Cut or tear the plants apart when their roots are intertwined.

If the ground is moist, merely open a hole with a trowel or dibble, insert the earth-incased roots of a plant, draw soil up to the stalk and firm with knuckles and the balls of thumbs. If the soil is at all dry, pour about a pint of water into each hole before the plant is set. The surface about each plant should be raked carefully when all the plants are set.

Transplanting (fig. 10) should be done if possible in cloudy weather or late in the afternoon. If the weather is especially bright it may be necessary for a day or two to shade the plants with news-

FIG. 10.—Transplanting stimulates branching root growth. Celery plants on the left were transplanted; those on right were not transplanted.

papers folded in inverted V shape and held in place with stones, earth, or other material.

The quickest crop to mature is the radish. Lettuce, turnips, peas, beets, and beans usually require 6 to 9 weeks to mature; cabbage, potatoes, early peas, onion sets, and salad greens, 10 to 12 weeks; corn from 11 to 13 weeks, and potatoes from 15 to 16 weeks.

SUCCESSIONS AND ROTATIONS.

Since a number of vegetables reach maturity early in the season, it is possible to utilize the space they occupied for successive plantings of the same vegetables or for rotation plantings of different plants. The earliest of all the vegetables to mature is the radish. The gardener generally can count on being able to utilize anew the space occupied by the first planting of these vegetables in from 5 to 7 weeks, depending on the rapidity with which they are consumed. In intensive gardening, however, it is not necessary to wait until all the radishes of the first planting have been removed before other plantings can be made. Enough of the roots can be removed at intervals to make places for setting lettuce, cabbage, cauliflower, Brussels sprouts, or other plants, and the two crops—radishes and the interplanted crop—can continue growing side by side until the former is used. In a similar way onion sets may be set out in rows that are to be occupied later by tomato plants, room being made for the latter by the removal of a few onions when the proper planting time for tomatoes arrives. Various combinations of this sort can be worked out between quick-maturing crops and the plants grown in frames or seed beds for later planting in the open.

The gardener should not plant all of his radish, lettuce, or spinach seed at once, but should make several successive plantings at intervals of about two weeks. In this way the season for these vegetables will be lengthened greatly. Successive planting is possible also with beets, peas, beans, sweet corn, and a number of other vegetables. The best of the successive crops of the quick-maturing vegetables must be crowded into the early part of the season, since most such plants do not thrive well when planted in hot weather. This is especially true of radishes and lettuce. In the case of lettuce this disadvantage can be overcome to a certain extent by artificial shading.

In all sections but the extreme north it usually is possible to grow fall crops of certain vegetables, notably carrots, beans, radishes, Irish potatoes, and turnips. In the southern part of the country an even larger number of vegetables may be grown in the fall. The seeds for these late crops are planted from July to September, depending on whether the garden is in the northern or southern States.

In planting rotations of crops, whether the rotations be during the same or in succeeding seasons, certain general principles should be kept in mind. In type and character of growth the succeeding plant should differ as widely as possible from the plant which it follows. This is both for the purpose of avoiding attacks by insects and diseases, and to insure that the second crop shall be properly nourished. A good plan is not to have root plants, such as beets and carrots, nor plants of the same family, such as cabbage and Brussels sprouts, or tomatoes and peppers, follow each other. It is well to divide the plants into root crops, fruiting crops, and foliage crops, and have members of the different groups alternate.

For the convenience of gardeners who wish to plan to use their soil to best advantage by means of successive plantings and rotations, the following groupings of vegetables are made:

1. Crops Occupying the Ground all Season.

Asparagus.	Salsify.	Eggplant.
Rhubarb.	Corn, late.	Peppers.
Beans, pole snap.	Cucumbers.	Onions (from seeds).
Beans, pole Lima.	Melons.	Leeks.
Beets, late.	Squash.	Okra.
Carrots, late.	Pumpkins.	Potatoes, main crop.
Parsnips.	Tomatoes.	Rutabagas.

2. Successive Crops.

Radish.	Peas.	Turnips.
Spinach.	Beans, dwarf.	Kohl-rabi.
Lettuce.	Parsley.	

3. Early Crops Which May be Followed by Others.[1]

Onion sets.	Turnips, early.	Corn, early.
Beets, early.	Carrots, early.	Cabbage, early.

4. Late Crops Which May Follow Others.[2]

Beets, late.	Cabbage, late.	Kale.
Spinach.	Brussels sprouts.	Endive.
Peas, late.	Cauliflower.	Flat turnips.
Celery.		

CULTIVATION.

The importance of cultivation has been referred to in the discussion of the preparation of the seed bed. It is, however, after the seeds have sprouted or after the plants have been set in their permanent locations that cultivation becomes of major importance. The gardener should never permit the surface of the soil to become baked or even to form an appreciable crust. Constant stirring with hand tools or a wheel cultivator should be practiced between the rows and about the plants. Such a stirring permits the air to penetrate the soil, where it facilitates chemical action and bacterial activity, destroys weeds which otherwise would utilize large amounts of plant food, and, finally, conserves the moisture supply. The rake is perhaps the gardener's most valuable tool in cultivating. This can be passed backward and forward over the ground until it is in an open, mellow condition. Where vegetables grow closely in the rows it often

---

[1] In addition to the vegetables listed in this group, all of those listed in Group II may be followed by other crops.
[2] Group II crops also may follow early crops.

will be necessary to supplement the cultivation by hand weeding. Small implements are made for this purpose, and may be purchased cheaply. It is well also in some cases to pull up weeds by hand, especially where they grow closely about the stalks of the garden plants.

STIRRING THE SOIL AFTER RAINS.

Just as the gardener should be careful in early spring not to dig the ground when the soil is too moist, so he should be careful later in the season not to cultivate too soon after rains. The stirring of very muddy soil "puddles" it into a compact, cement-like mass in which the plant food is securely locked. The garden will require attention, however, as soon as the excess moisture from a rain has soaked in or partially evaporated. Unless the ground is stirred at this time a crust will form almost inevitably. Such a crust, besides restricting the plants, prevents the access of air, and also facilitates the loss of moisture through evaporation.

IRRIGATION.

When, during prolonged dry spells, the plants give evidence of suffering because of the lack of moisture, water must, if possible, be supplied artificially. Where a supply of piped water is at hand, perhaps the most usual method of irrigation is by sprinkling with a hose. If sprinkling is practiced it should be done late in the afternoon. It is not sufficient merely to dampen the surface; a thorough wetting should be given. A more satisfactory and more economical method of irrigation, however, is to open small furrows between the rows of growing plants and to supply water in these ditches from a hose or pipe. Several hours after the water has soaked in, the dry earth should be drawn back into place.

PROTECTING PLANTS FROM DISEASES AND PESTS.

Unfortunately the gardener is not assured of success when his plants have started to grow thriftily. He must count almost inevitably upon the presence in his garden of plant diseases and pests, which, if not combated, will interfere seriously with his yields or even destroy his plants. It is hard for some gardeners to realize the importance of making early provision to combat these enemies of plant life. It can not be too strongly emphasized, however, that such provision is of equal importance with other phases of gardening and that it should under no circumstances be neglected. The wise gardener does not wait for the appearance of insects and diseases, but takes steps to combat them by spraying the plants at reasonable intervals from early spring until his crops have been harvested, or by other protective measures. He thus insures himself against the likelihood of loss.

The necessary implements and materials for protecting the home garden against insects and diseases should be assembled early in the season. These consist of a substantial hand sprayer and the necessary concentrated solutions, which, after dilution with water, are to be sprayed on the plants.

The diseases which affect garden plants may be divided into two groups, parasitic and constitutional diseases. The parasitic maladies, such as the blights, are caused by fungi or germs, and usually may be prevented or controlled by spraying with Bordeaux mixture. Little is known, however, of the so-called constitutional diseases, and little can be done to prevent their ravages. If some malady which does not yield to treatment with Bordeaux mixture manifests itself on isolated plants in the garden, it may be well to pull up these plants and burn them.

The insects which attack garden plants may be divided into two groups—those which eat or chew the fruit or foliage, and those which suck the plant juices. Eating insects may be killed usually by spraying poisonous solutions or dusting powders on the plants which they attack. Arsenate of lead is the poison in most general use for this purpose. This substance is poisonous to persons as well as to insects and must be used with care. It should not be applied to vegetables that are to be used soon. All vegetables should be washed carefully before they are eaten, regardless of whether they have been sprayed.

Most of the garden plants may be guarded against disease and at the same time protected from attack by eating insects by spraying at intervals of two weeks with a combination of Bordeaux mixture and arsenate of lead.

Other methods of protecting plants from the larger eating insects are to pick the pests by hand or knock them with a stick into a pan containing water on which a thin film of kerosene is floating. Insects collected by hand should be destroyed promptly. Young plants may be protected by setting over them wooden frames covered with mosquito netting, wire mesh, or cheesecloth. Cutworms may be kept from plants by setting tin or paper collars into the ground around the stalks.

Sucking insects, such as plant lice, can not be killed by poisoning the surface of the leaves and fruit, since they feed by puncturing the plants and extracting the internal juices. Poisons which will kill by contact or substances which envelop and smother the pests are, therefore, employed against the sucking insects. The principal remedies of this sort are nicotine solutions, fish-oil and other soap solutions, and kerosene emulsion.

The following table lists the insects most likely to appear in the vegetable garden and furnishes information in regard to the plants attacked and the treatment recommended:

Principal insects and remedies.[1]

Insect.	Plants attacked.	Treatment.
Eating type:		
Tomato worms......	Tomato..................	Hand pick or spray with arsenate of lead.
Cabbage worm......	Cabbage group.............	Hand pick or apply arsenate of lead.
Cucumber beetles...	Cucumber.................	Cover with frames. Apply tobacco dust or spray with Bordeaux mixture or arsenate of lead.
Cutworms..........	Tomato, cabbage, onion......	Apply poison bait; place tin or paper collars around plants; hand pick; apply Paris green or arsenate of lead.
Potato beetle.......	Potato, eggplant, and tomato	Hand pick and apply arsenate of lead.
Sucking type:		
Squash bug.........	Squash, pumpkin, melons, etc.	Hand pick; spray with kerosene emulsion or nicotine sulphate.
Aphis (plant lice)...	Cabbage group and other plants.	Spray with kerosene emulsion, a solution of hard soap, or nicotine sulphate.

Gardeners desiring additional information in regard to insects affecting the vegetable garden should apply direct to the Bureau of Entomology, United States Department of Agriculture, but it should be understood that there is no publication covering the entire subject. Specimens of insects with some account of food plants and ravages should accompany correspondence.

The gardener should remember that many plant diseases and insects exist in the garden from year to year. At the end of the growing season, therefore, the garden should be carefully cleaned of rubbish, the

Fig. 11.—Head lettuce produces very tender, almost white leaves in the center of the heads, but is somewhat harder to grow than the loose-leaf sorts.

stems of plants, leaves, etc. It is necessary to burn this débris promptly, as any disease spores or insects which may be present are then surely destroyed.

[1] Methods of protecting gardens against grasshoppers are given in Farmers' Bulletin 691, "Grasshoppers and Their Control on Sugar Beets and Truck Crops."

Fig. 12.—Loose-leaf or open-headed lettuce is excellent for growing in the home garden, since its cultural requirements are not so exacting as those of head lettuce.

CULTURAL SUGGESTIONS FOR THE COMMONER VEGETABLES.

RADISH.

Radishes are so hardy that they may be grown through the winter in cold frames in the latitude of Washington and farther South in the open ground. In the North they require hotbeds, but can be sown in the open ground as soon as the soil is moderately warm. They should be planted in drills 12 to 18 inches apart and thinned slightly as soon as the plants are up. On a quick, rich soil some of the earlier varieties can be matured in from three to four weeks after planting. If the plants are allowed to remain long in the open ground, the roots lose their crispness and delicate flavor, and in order to secure a constant supply successive plantings should be made every two weeks. One ounce of radish seed is sufficient to plant 100 feet of row. A large percentage of the seed germinates, and if the sowing is done carefully later thinning may be unnecessary. The first radishes to appear may be pulled as soon as they are of sufficient size, and this will leave enough room for those that are a little later. The plant is not suited to hot weather, but should be planted in the early spring and late autumn.

LETTUCE.

Lettuce does not withstand heat well and thrives best, therefore, in the early spring or late autumn. In order to have the leaves crisp and tender it is necessary to force the growth of the plant. The usual method of growing lettuce for home use is to sow the seeds broadcast in the bed and to remove the leaves as rapidly as they become large enough for use. It is better, however, to sow the seeds in rows 14 to 16 inches apart, and when the plants come up to thin them to the desired distance. With the heading type this should be about 12 inches apart. This will result in the formation of rather compact heads and the entire plant may then be cut for use. For an early crop in the North, the plants should be started in a hotbed or cold frame and transplanted as soon as hard freezes are over. In many sections of the South the seeds are sown during the autumn and the plant allowed to remain in the ground over winter. Frequent shallow cultivation should be given the crop and, if crisp, tender lettuce is desired during the summer months, some form of partial shading may be necessary.

For head lettuce (fig. 11), Big Boston, Hanson, and California Cream Butter are good varieties. For loose-leaf lettuce (fig. 12), Grand Rapids or Black-seeded Simpson is recommended.

PEAS.

Garden peas are not injured easily by light frosts and may be planted as soon as the soil can be put in order in the spring. By selecting a number of varieties it is possible to have a continuous supply of peas throughout a large portion of the growing season. In order to accomplish this plantings should be made every 10 days or 2 weeks until warm weather comes. The first plantings should be of small-growing, quick-maturing varieties, such as Alaska, First and Best, and Gradus. These kinds do not require supports. They

Fig. 13.—Tall-growing garden peas supported by brush stuck into the ground.

should be followed by the large wrinkled type of peas, such as Champion of England, Telephone, and Prize Taker. These may be supported on brush (fig. 13), on strings attached to stakes driven in the ground, or on wire netting.

Peas should be planted about 2 to 3 inches deep in rows 3 to 4 feet apart. Some gardeners, however, follow the practice of planting in double rows 6 inches apart, with the ordinary space of 3 to 4 feet between these pairs of rows. With varieties requiring support this is a good practice, as the supports can be placed in the narrow space between the rows.

ONIONS.

The onion will thrive under a wide range of climate and soil conditions, but a rich sandy loam containing plenty of humus is best suited to it. (Fig. 14.) As the crop requires shallow cultivation and it may be necessary to resort to hand work in order to keep it free from weeds, it is very desirable that the land should be in such condition that it is easily worked. As a general rule it is well to have the crop follow some other that has been kept under the hoe and free from weeds the previous season.

In the North seed is sown as early in the spring as the soil

FIG. 14.—Onions are easily grown on good soil and require little attention besides weeding.

can be brought to the proper condition. In the South onion sets are frequently put out in the autumn and carried through the winter with the protection of a little hay or straw. There are three methods of propagating onions: The first by sowing the seed in rows where the crop is to grow; second, by sowing the seed in specially prepared beds and transplanting the seedlings to the open ground; and, third, by planting sets which have been kept through the winter. The first method is used by large commercial growers on account of the amount of labor involved in the others.

On small areas, however, it may be preferable to plant sets. Under normal conditions these usually may be obtained at planting time for about 25 or 30 cents a quart. This should be enough for the average family. Onions planted from sets will ripen earlier than those from seed sown in the fields.

When the transplanting method is used, the seed is sown in greenhouses, hotbeds, cold frames, or specially prepared beds at the rate of $3\frac{1}{2}$ to 4 pounds for each acre to be planted. One-half ounce should furnish plants sufficient for the home garden. The seedlings are transplanted when they are somewhat smaller than a lead pencil and rather stocky. The root end of the seedling is pushed into the soil with one finger, and the soil is then firmed about the plant.

The seed is sown thickly in drills about 12 to 14 inches apart. After the plants become established they are thinned to 2 or 3 inches apart. The maturity of the bulbs may be hastened by preventing the continued growth of the tops. This is sometimes accomplished by rolling an empty barrel over the rows and breaking down the tops. After these are practically dead the onion bulbs may be pulled up by hand from the soil and spread in a dry, well-ventilated place to cure. Thereafter they may be stored in crates or bags for winter use. In the North the crop ripens and is harvested during the latter part of the summer and early autumn. In the Southern States, where the crop is grown during the winter, the harvesting and marketing period takes place during the spring months.

There are several kinds of onions that may remain in the soil over winter. The multiplier, or potato onion, for example, can be planted from sets in the autumn and will produce excellent green early onions. A large onion of this type contains a number of distinct hearts, and, if planted, will produce a number of small onions. On the other hand, a small onion contains but one heart and will produce a large onion. A few of the large ones may be planted each year to produce sets for the following year's planting.

The shallot is a variety of small onion that is frequently planted in early spring for its small bulbs, or "cloves," which are used in the same manner as onions. The leaves are utilized for flavoring. Another onion-like plant is the chive, the small, round, hollow leaves of which are used for flavoring soups. These leaves may be cut freely, as they are soon replaced by others.

THE PRINCIPAL ROOT CROPS.

Beets (fig. 15) can be planted comparatively early in the season. It is not necessary to wait until the ground has become warm, if the danger of frost is past. The seed should be sown in drills 14 to 18 inches apart and covered to a depth of about 1 inch. As soon as the plants are well up they should be thinned to stand 3 to 4 inches apart. From 2 to 3 plantings should be made in order to have a continuous supply of young, tender beets.

Parsnips, salsify, carrots, and turnips are all handled much like beets. Of the five, carrots can perhaps be left closer in the row than the others, about 2 or 3 inches apart. This plant, too, is less exacting in so far as fertility is concerned. Salsify, on the other hand, demands very fertile and finely cultivated soil.

POTATOES.[1]

The potato plant thrives best in sandy or gravelly loam soils. It may be grown with a fair degree of success on any type of soil except loose sand and a heavy, sticky clay, provided the land is well drained and contains the necessary plant food.

Successful potato production is dependent to a large extent on the thoroughness with which the land is prepared before planting the crop. Where a horse can be used, the land should be plowed from 8 to 10 inches deep, provided the surface soil is of a sufficient depth to permit it. It is never advisable to turn up more than 1 inch of raw subsoil at any one plowing; so if previous plowings have not been over 6 inches, the maximum depth at which it should be plowed is 7 inches.

Where hand labor is employed the same rule should govern as to depth. In spading, especially on grass or waste land, turn the earth bottom side up.

FIG. 15.—Both the roots and foliage of young beets may be eaten, cooked together or separately.

Whether the land is plowed or spaded, it should be thoroughly pulverized immediately afterwards. Where horse labor can be used, the land after plowing should be thoroughly disked first, then spring-toothed, and finally finished with a smoothing harrow. Where land must be prepared by hand, it is good practice to pulverize the soil as much as possible when spading it up, after which it can be put in a fine condition of mellowness with a steel garden rake. The importance of thoroughly fining the soil can not be overemphasized.

VARIETIES ADAPTED TO DIFFERENT LOCALITIES.

Early varieties.—In the Northeastern United States and along the South Atlantic seaboard, the Irish Cobbler, Early Petoskey, or Early

---

[1] Circular 87 of the Bureau of Entomology deals with the Colorado potato beetle, and Farmers' Bulletin 557 deals with the Potato tuber moth.

Standard, all of which are practically identical, may be expected to produce larger crops and be more generally satisfactory for an early crop than the others mentioned. Quick Lunch and New Queen would be regarded as second choices for this section.

In the South Central and Southwestern States, the Triumph may be expected to give results equal to or even better than the Irish Cobbler.

In the Middle West, the Early Ohio should do well, while the Early Harvest and Early Rose may be regarded as second choices.

Late varieties.—In the New England States, Long Island, and northern New York, the Green Mountain, Gold Coin, Delaware, and other late varieties of that class do best.

In northern Michigan, Wisconsin, and Minnesota, the late varieties named above do about as well as the Rural New Yorker No. 2, and are superior to it in table quality.

In western New York, southern Michigan and Wisconsin, and Iowa, the Rural New Yorker No. 2, Sir Walter Raleigh, and Carman No. 3 are the best adapted varieties, and divide honors with the Green Mountain in the northern portions of these States.

Throughout Maryland, Virginia, the Carolinas, Tennessee, and Georgia, the variety known as McCormick is quite generally grown as a late variety. In a favorable season the Green Mountain can also be grown.

WHEN TO PLANT POTATOES.

The date of planting necessarily must be governed by climatic conditions. In attempting to produce as early a crop as possible some risk must always be incurred of the plants being injured by late spring frosts. As a general proposition it is best to plant potatoes as soon as there is little likelihood of killing frosts after the plants are up and the ground is in condition to work.

The following dates of planting for various cities should be regarded only as the approximate time at which early potatoes might safely be planted:

March 15 to 25: Washington, Baltimore, Philadelphia, Cincinnati, Louisville, St. Louis.

March 25 to April 5: New York, Indianapolis, Detroit, Chicago.

April 5 to 15: Boston, Albany, Rochester, etc.

In the northern cities late varieties should be planted from three to four weeks later.

PLANTING PRACTICES.

The usual method of preparing potatoes for planting is to cut them into rather large pieces, containing several eyes. When seed potatoes are unusually expensive, however, it may be well to cut cone-shaped segments of meat around each eye and to use the remaining portion of the tubers for food. Under this plan it is not necessary to prepare the seed all at one time. From day to day the cones for seeding can be cut from the potatoes as they are being prepared for the table. The cuttings then should be spread out on a piece of paper in a moderately cool room (about 50° F.) and allowed to remain there until they have cured; that is, until the cut surface has become dry. A day or two should suffice for this, and potatoes then should be put in a shallow box or tray and placed where it is still cooler. Any storage condition that will insure them against frost on the one hand and undue shriveling on the other should prove satisfactory.

These seeds can be started indoors, provided it is possible to secure suitable soil and boxes. In such cases it may be desirable to plant the eye cuttings at once, and allow them to start into growth indoors with the idea of transplanting them into the open ground when danger of frost is past and the ground is dry enough to be cultivated.

The smaller the size of the set, or seed piece, used the more thorough must be the preparation of the soil. The more finely the soil is pulverized and the more uniform the moisture conditions which can be preserved in the soil, the better is the chance for the small seed piece to establish itself. A small set in rough, lumpy, or dried-out soil has little chance to live.

Generally speaking, the smaller the size of the set the closer it should be planted in the row if maximum yields are to be secured. Such sets may be expected to give the best yields if not spaced more than 10 to 12 inches apart in the row. Plant the small eye cuttings from 1½ to 3 inches deep, depending upon the character of the soil— the lighter the soil the greater the depth of planting. Larger sets may be planted 4 inches deep.

SPACING.

If an early variety is planted, and the work is to be done by hand, the rows may be spaced as close as 26 inches, whereas if cultivation is to be done with a horse, 30 to 34 inches usually is allowed. In order to give the gardener some idea of the number of sets required to plant a plot of ground 50 by 100 feet at different spacings, the following table is submitted:

To plant a plat 50 by 100 feet.

Space between rows.	Space in row between plants.	Sets required.	Space between rows.	Space in row between plants.	Sets required.
Inches.	Inches.		Inches.	Inches.	
26	10	2,769	30	10	2,400
26	12	2,487	30	12	2,000
28	10	2,678	32	12	1,874
28	12	2,231	34	12	1,765

If a late variety is planted, the spacing should be greater, say, 34 to 36 inches between the rows and 12 to 14 inches between the plants in the row. The closeness of planting should be determined, first, by the variety, and, second, by the amount of available plant food and moisture in the soil or that can be applied to it.

CORN.

Corn (fig. 16) to be at its best should be eaten within a few hours after it is picked, for its sugar content disappears very rapidly after it is removed from the garden. For this reason and because of its very general popularity it is an excellent vegetable to grow in the home garden. It should be planted on rich land and cultivated in the same manner as field corn. Beginning as soon as the soil is warm, successive plantings may be made every two or three weeks until late summer. Another method of prolonging the supply is to plant early, medium, and late varieties. The seed should be planted about

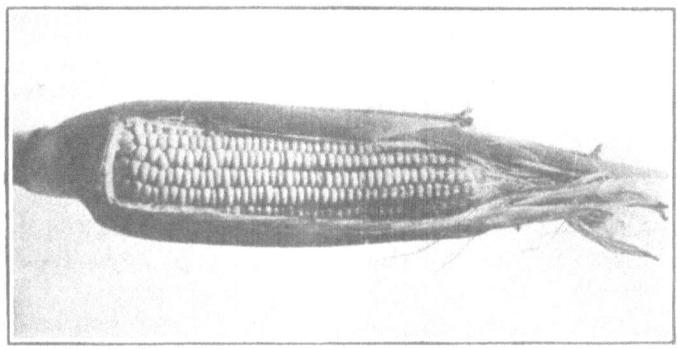

FIG. 16.—Green corn is one of the vegetables which loses much of its flavor if kept long after it is cut before being eaten. It should, therefore, be grown in the home garden if space permits.

2 inches deep, in drills 3 feet apart, and thinned to a single stalk every 10 to 14 inches.

The following varieties are recommended: For early corn, Golden Bantam and Adams Early, and for medium and late varieties, Black Mexican or Crosby's Early, Country Gentleman, and Stowell's Evergreen. The last-named variety has the largest ears and is the most productive.

Corn should be planted on rich land. The cultivation should be frequent and thorough and all weeds should be kept down and suckers removed from around the base of the plant.

TOMATOES.

Tomato plants should be started in the house or in a hotbed and should be transplanted once or twice in order that strong and vigorous plants may be secured by the time all danger from frost is past.

Fig. 17.—Tomato vines tied to stakes produce cleaner, healthier fruit than those permitted to trail on the ground, and giving the garden a more attractive appearance. The stakes need not be so large as those here pictured.

Pot-grown plants are especially desirable, as they may be brought to the blooming period by the time it is warm enough to plant them with safety in the garden. If the plants are not to be trained (fig. 17), but are to be allowed to lie on the ground, they should be set about 4 feet apart each way. If trimmed and tied to stakes they may be planted in rows 3 feet apart and 18 inches apart in the row. The home gardener will find the latter method preferable.

In common with all plants grown in a house, hotbed, or cold frame, tomatoes require to be hardened off before they are planted in the garden. By this process the plants are gradually acclimated to the effects of the sun and wind, so that they will stand transplanting to the open ground. Hardening off usually is accomplished by ventilating freely and by reducing the amount of water applied to the plant bed. The bed, however, should not become so dry that the plants will wilt or become seriously checked in their growth. After a few days it will be possible to leave the plants uncovered during the entire day and on mild nights.

EGGPLANTS AND PEPPERS.

Eggplants (fig. 18) and peppers are started and handled in the same way as the tomato. The soil best adapted for their production is a fine, rich sandy loam, well drained. The plants should be set in rows 3 feet apart and 2 feet apart in the row. Free cultivation is desirable, and the plants should be kept growing rapidly. A dozen good healthy plants each of eggplant and pepper should supply enough fruits for the average sized family throughout the season. Both of these vegetables are heat-loving and should not be set in the open until the ground has become warm.

BEANS.

Beans are more susceptible to cold than peas and should not be planted until danger of frost is past and the ground begins to warm up. They are, however, among the most desirable vegetables that the home gardener can raise. There are many different kinds and varieties of beans, but for garden purposes they may be divided into two classes—string and Lima. Both classes are grown in practically all parts of the United States where the frost-free period is greater than three months and adapt themselves to a wide diversity of soils and climate. They grow rapidly and, therefore, leave the area in which they have been planted free for another crop. To secure a continuous supply, it is desirable to make plantings at

FIG. 18.—When grown under good soil and cultural conditions the eggplant is a prolific yielder. All the fruits shown in this illustration are on a single plant.

Fig. 19.—Pole lima beans are prolific bearers, as the illustration shows. Like other beans, they thrive on almost any soil. Vegetables that may be trained on poles or fences help to economize space in the small garden.

intervals of 10 days or 2 weeks from the time that the ground is reasonably warm until hot weather sets in.

Both string and Lima beans are subdivided into pole and bush types. Pole Lima beans (fig. 19) should be planted with from 8 to

10 seeds in the hill, and after the plants become established should be thinned to 3 or 4. The hills should be 4 or 5 feet apart. Bush Lima beans are planted 5 or 6 inches apart in rows 30 to 36 inches apart. Bush beans of the string type may be planted somewhat closer—the plants standing 3 or 4 inches apart in rows from 20 to 24 inches apart if hand cultivation only is to be employed.

Beans of any kind should not be planted any deeper than is necessary to secure good germination. This should never be over 2 inches and on heavy soil it should not be more than 1¼ to 1½ inches.

Beans are useful in the home garden, since they thrive on practically any type of soil. The pole varieties are especially convenient, since they can be planted along the edges of the yard and permitted to climb on the fences. Some of the pole beans, both snap and Lima, will continue to bear until frost. If the pole beans are planted in the hills in the garden proper, it will be necessary to sink a pole at each hill or to provide some other form of support. Extra long poles may be used and the tops of three or four from different hills fastened together tent fashion.

FIG. 20.—Hubbard squash vines occupy considerable space but may be grown in the larger home gardens.

If it is desired to keep the garden free from poles, substantial posts may be set at each end of the row and a wire or strong cord stretched between their tops. Cords may then be extended from small stakes in each hill to the wire.

CUCUMBERS, SQUASHES, AND MELONS.

Cucumbers, squashes[1] (fig. 20), and melons all belong to the melon family and demand much the same treatment. All are heat-loving and should not be planted in the open until the ground has become warm. It is easily possible, however, to give the plants an early start in the house and so gain several weeks in earliness of maturity. One way is to plant seven or eight seeds in berry boxes filled with soil. Each box of growing plants should have its bottom removed at planting time and should then be sunk in the garden to constitute a hill of plants.

Instead of growing the plants in boxes of ordinary soil they may be grown on sods in a suitable receptacle. Cut sods 6 inches square

---

[1] An insect that attacks squashes and other crops of this class is described in Farmers' Bulletin 668, "The Squash-vine Borer."

from spots which the growth of grass shows to be rich. Turn these grass side down and press the seeds in among the roots and soil. Cover with about an inch and a half of good soil and keep moist and warm. At planting time the sods may be lifted and placed in hills, which first should have manure worked into them.

These plants are rank growers and occupy much space. In very small gardens it may be well, therefore, to omit them. If squashes are grown, it may be well to plant only bunch varieties. Space may be conserved by growing a few cucumber vines near the edge of the garden and training them on a fence. This is possible, too, of course, with some melons and pumpkins, but supports will be necessary for the fruits. If the plants of this group are grown in the main garden, they must be spaced from 6 to 12 feet apart each way.

CABBAGE, CAULIFLOWER, AND BRUSSELS SPROUTS.

Cabbage and the other two members of the cabbage family mentioned here require much the same treatment.[1] All three are grown in hotbeds, frames, or flats for the early crop and are set out when all danger of frost is past. Of the three, Brussels sprouts (fig. 21) is the hardiest. Cabbage is fairly hardy, but cauliflower is somewhat tender. All require rather moist soil and plenty of plant food. Fertilizer may be conserved by placing it under each "hill" before the plants are set. The settings should be made 18 to 24 inches apart in rows spaced about 24 inches.

FIG. 21.—A single plant of Brussels sprouts. The miniature "heads" on the stalk are cut off and cooked like cabbage.

MISCELLANEOUS SALAD VEGETABLES.

Besides lettuce there are a number of vegetables for use as salads or cooked greens that may be grown easily in the home garden. Of the salad plants corn salad, garden cress, and endive are perhaps best known. The first two may be planted early. Endive, however,

---

[1] Accounts of two insects that attack cabbage are given in Farmers' Bulletin 766, "The Common Cabbage Worm," and Circular 103 of the Bureau of Entomology, "The Harlequin Cabbage Bug."

is planted in June and July. All are grown in drills about 14 inches apart and are thinned to proper distances as they grow.

Spinach and mustard are useful greens for cooking. Spinach may be grown either in the spring or in the fall. It is grown in drills, the use of the larger plants first automatically taking care of thinning.

Mustard greens may be produced on almost any good soil. The basal leaves are used for greens and are cooked like spinach. The plants require but a short time to reach the proper stage for use and frequent sowings should be made. The seeds are sowed thickly in drills as early as possible in spring or for late use in September or October. Ostrich Plume is a reliable variety.

For use both as a salad plant and for cooked greens Swiss chard (fig. 22), a beet which has been developed for foliage, should be more extensively grown. One of the good points about this vegetable is that crop after crop of leaves may be cut without injuring the plant. Chard is planted like beets in drills 12 to 14 inches apart and thinned to 4 to 6 inches.

PERMANENT VEGETABLES.

A number of vegetables, once established, will furnish a supply of their products year after year. Asparagus, rhubarb, and a number of garnishing and flavoring herbs are the best-known members of this group. Because they permanently occupy the space in which they grow, such plants should be in beds separated from the cultivated vegetables.

Fig. 22.—Swiss chard, a beet which has been bred for salad foliage instead of for root. The leaves and stalks may be cut repeatedly and used like spinach. Since the plant furnishes salad greens throughout the season it may well be grown instead of spinach, which furnishes but one crop, or after spinach.

For the asparagus bed a well drained, early location should be chosen. Prepare the bed by digging a trench 18 inches wide and 20 inches deep. Fill this one-third full with well-rotted manure and tramp it down well. Half fill the remaining space with good soil, and on this set the root clumps of asparagus, 1 foot apart. Such roots, one, two, or three years old, may be purchased from seedsmen or nurseries. Cover the roots by filling the trench to the surface of the ground with good soil. The stalks should not be cut until a year after planting, and then but lightly. Full harvests may be taken after this. From a dozen to two dozen roots should be enough for the average family.

Rhubarb is also grown from root clumps. A row of six or eight plants, 4 feet apart, should furnish stalks enough for the average family. Each hill should be well prepared with manure and good soil. Set the crowns about 4 inches underground. Stalks should not be cut until a year after planting.

Parsley seeds are sown in a drill in spring. The plants will die down in the fall and put out fresh foliage the next spring. The plant is a biennial and must be replanted at two-year intervals.

Sage is a useful perennial herb which can be grown easily in the home garden. One or two bushes will furnish an abundance of leaves. These, when full grown, should be thoroughly dried and stored in cans or jars.

ANNUAL PLANTS USED FOR SEASONING.

Chives are small onionlike plants having flat, hollow leaves. These are cut and used for flavoring soups, sauces, etc. The plants are propagated by bulbs. A patch of the plants a foot or so square should be enough for the home garden.

Okra, or gumbo, produces pods which are used to season and thicken soups. The seeds of okra should be sown in the open after the ground has become quite warm, or the plants may be started in berry boxes in the hotbed or in the house and transplanted in the garden after all danger of frost has passed. The rows should be 4 feet apart for the dwarf sorts and 5 feet apart for the tall kinds, with the plants 2 feet apart in the row.[1] If the pods are removed before they are allowed to ripen, the plants will continue to produce them until killed by frost.

Cabbage, carrots, turnips, and rutabagas, in addition to their use as early crops, may be planted early in summer and the products which mature in autumn may then be held for winter use.

---

[1] Detailed information on this plant is contained in Farmers' Bulletin 232, "Okra: Its Culture and Uses."

VEGETABLES FOR WINTER USE.

For a late crop of cabbage it is customary to plant the seeds in a bed in the open ground in May or June and transplant them to the garden in July. For cabbage of this character the soil should be heavier and more retentive of moisture than for early cabbage, which requires a rich, warm soil in order to reach maturity quickly. For the late variety it is not desirable to have too rich a soil, as the heads are liable to burst. Cabbages should be set in rows 30 to 36 inches apart, the plants standing 14 to 18 inches apart in the row.

To store cabbage for winter the heads should be buried in pits or placed in cellars. One method is to dig a trench about 18 inches deep and 3 feet wide and set the cabbage upright with the heads close together and the roots embedded in the soil. When cold weather comes the heads are covered lightly with straw and 3 or 4 inches of earth put in. Slight freezing does not injure cabbage, but it should not be subjected to repeated freezing and thawing.

Parsnips will occupy the ground from early spring until fall. The seeds should be sown as early as convenient in the spring in rows 18 inches to 3 feet apart. The plants should later be thinned to stand 3 inches apart in the row. A rich soil with frequent cultivation is necessary for success with this crop. The roots are dug late in the fall and stored in cellars or pits, much as cabbage is, or else are allowed to remain where they are grown and are dug as required for use. All roots not dug during the winter, however, should be removed from the garden, as they will produce seed the second season and become of a weedy nature. When the parsnip has been allowed to run wild in this way the root is considered to be poisonous.

Carrots may be sown early, used during the late summer, and the surplus stored. If desired, a later crop may be sown after the removal of an early vegetable, especially for winter use. Carrots are grown in practically the same way as parsnips, but are not thinned so much and are allowed to grow almost as thickly as planted. They are dug in the autumn and stored in the same manner as parsnips or turnips.

Turnips require a rich soil and may be grown either as an early or late crop. For a late crop it is customary to sow the seeds broadcast on land from which some early crop has been removed. In the North this is generally done during July and August, but the usual time is later in the South. The seed also may be sown in drills 12 to 18 inches apart as for the early crop. After the plants appear they are thinned to about 3 inches.

The rutabaga is similar to the turnip and is grown in much the same way. It requires more space, however, and a longer period for its growth. It is used to a considerable extent for stock feed and has the advantage of being quite hardy.

FRUITS IN THE SMALL GARDEN.

BERRIES.

If there is sufficient space in the home garden, it may be desirable to have it supply fruits as well as vegetables. The small fruits, such as strawberries, raspberries, blackberries, currants, and gooseberries, may be produced with little trouble. A few dozen strawberry plants, and even fewer of the other plants mentioned, should be sufficient for a start. The plantings can be increased from year to year by resetting the young plants which spring up from runners and roots. All the small fruit plants mentioned may be set out in spring. Since most of these plants will occupy the same space year after year, they should be segregated from the part of the garden devoted to annual vegetables.

Grapes may, in many instances, be grown in the home garden more easily than the small bush fruits, since they may be planted near fences and permitted to run upon them. Grape plants also may be set out in spring before the sap rises. Fairly large holes should be dug, and these filled with rich soil mixed with wood ashes.

TREE FRUITS.

Tree fruits probably can not be grown in most small home gardens because of the relatively large areas of soil their roots occupy. The use of dwarf trees, however, makes possible the growing of a few fruit trees in the larger yards and garden inclosures. Though strawberries, cucumbers, and a few other vegetables may be grown near the trees while the latter are small, most vegetables must be grown in the open, where they will receive abundant sunlight. If fruit trees are grown in connection with gardening operations, therefore, they should, where possible, be well removed from the main garden plot.

Apple, peach, cherry, pear, plum, apricot, and quince trees may be purchased on dwarfing stocks. All may be set out in the spring before growth starts. The trees should be set in holes several feet square in which rich soil has been placed. They should be set an inch or so lower than in the nursery.

○

U. S. DEPARTMENT OF AGRICULTURE
FARMERS' BULLETIN No. 1733

PLANNING A SUBSISTENCE HOMESTEAD

MANY FAMILIES with small incomes can lower their living costs by living on a small piece of land and growing their own food, and at the same time enjoy a greater quantity and variety of fresh and canned vegetables and fruit. Gardening and poultry raising on a small piece of land is about all an employed man and his family can care for by hand. About 1 acre of good land is enough for such purposes.

But if the family wants to keep a cow and plans to buy the necessary winter feed, 2 acres of good pasture land, in addition, should be enough, and the extra work will not be excessive.

Men employed only part time or short hours who have large families and small incomes may find it economical to keep a milk cow, or milk goats, and some pigs, and raise the necessary feed in addition to having a garden and keeping poultry. This plan means the use of horse or mechanical power and should be tried only after experience and careful consideration.

Some families are so placed that their best plan involves obtaining a fairly large acreage of cheap land for general farming. In many areas this cheap land is extremely poor and has failed to yield a reasonable living under any kind of farming. For this reason extreme care must be exercised in selecting a so-called cheap farm.

Washington, D. C.   Issued May 1934
                                Slightly revised April 1940

PLANNING A SUBSISTENCE HOMESTEAD

By WALTER W. WILCOX, *junior agricultural economist, Division of Farm Management and Costs, Bureau of Agricultural Economics* [1]

CONTENTS

	Page		Page
Renewal of interest	1	Feed and livestock production on a subsistence homestead	12
Selecting land near cities	2	The family cow	12
Vegetable, poultry, and fruit production	3	Milk goats	14
Lay-out for a small acreage	3	Pork for family use	14
Quantity and variety of garden vegetables and small fruits	5	Feed for livestock on small acreages	16
The small poultry flock	7	Possibilities of a small wood lot	17
Production of tree fruits on small acreages	8	Limitations of small acreages as a means of self-support	17
Fertilizers	9	Production for home use on larger acreages	18
Insects, diseases, and other handicaps	9	Self-sufficing farms	18
Cash expenses for agricultural production and returns	10	Individual farms vary in productivity	18
Winter vegetable and fruit supply for a family of five	10	Farmers' bulletins of interest	19

RENEWAL OF INTEREST

GROWING FOOD for family-living purposes in connection with enough outside work to provide the family with the cash for necessary farm and family expenses is a combination that many families now want to develop. Recent hard times and still more recent Governmental policies have renewed an intensified interest in this possible combination. This kind of farming has often been called subsistence farming and a farm of this kind a subsistence homestead.

This part-time farming has certain problems of its own that are somewhat different from the usual farming problems. The family has to think of the quantity and variety of products it needs rather than of what the markets demand. Those who are inexperienced often overestimate the savings made possible by this way of living, and they often underestimate the costs in the way of the labor and cash necessary in such part-time farming.

In this kind of farming special attention is given to obtaining just the right area and kind of land; for when much of the work is done by hand, a heavy soil that is hard to work is a great disadvantage. With no power available, and with only a minimum of livestock, keeping unused land free from weeds is a burden.

[1] Members of the staff of the Division of Subsistence Homesteads, U.S. Department of the Interior, assisted in preparing this publication including its illustrations. W. R. Beattie, senior horticulturist, Bureau of Plant Industry, worked out the detailed plans for the garden and fruit production on the small acreages, and Medora M. Ward, assistant economist, Economics Division, Bureau of Home Economics, supplied the section regarding the winter vegetable and fruit supply for a family of five.

This combination of farming and wage work off the farm, now usually called subsistence farming, is particularly attractive to those families with several children who find it difficult to provide suitable housing and plenty of fresh fruits and vegetables from their small incomes. It is much less attractive if wages from work off the farm are not enough to meet the necessary cash expenses of the farm and the family living. Inexperienced people will find severe competition if they try to raise farm products for sale.

Many people now in town who lived on farms in their childhood inquire about subsistence or "self-sufficing" farming on 20 to 100 acres or more. Many farms that are apparently suitable for such a purpose are now for sale at relatively low prices, but many serious problems are involved in this kind of farming. Only a few of those problems are discussed here as most of them are covered in other Farmers' Bulletins, a brief list of which is given at the end of this bulletin.

This bulletin deals chiefly with the economic problems that will be met by those people who are planning to combine part-time farming and wage earning.

SELECTING LAND NEAR CITIES

Several problems are involved in selecting a small piece of land near a city in which jobs may be found. The first is the difference in the prices of land with reference to location. The price of land near a city is often based as much on residential value as on productive capacity. Two tracts of land equally valuable from the point of view of building sites may not be equally valuable for use in growing fruits and vegetables. A part-time farmer should have good, productive land. The importance of the soil cannot be overemphasized. A moderately level, fertile, well-drained piece of land that is free from stones and can be readily worked may easily be worth twice as much as another nearby tract of the same size. Sandy loam soils usually can be worked earlier in the spring than the stiff clay loams, but crops on the clay loams frequently withstand dry weather better than those on lighter soils. By draining, irrigating, manuring, and the right kind of cultivating any reasonably good soil can be made suitable for the intensive growing of vegetables.

Distance to place of employment and transportation facilities are other important considerations. Studies show that most part-time farmers do not want to drive more than 10 miles to work. Other things being equal, a location near several places where jobs might be found has many advantages over a location where a family would be rather cut off if the one industrial plant closed down.

If city water is not available at a reasonable cost, a good supply of pure well or spring water is necessary. A small tract of land that is otherwise suitable for a subsistence homestead may not have a supply of pure water available because of surface or underground drainage. Public health authorities in the nearby city will test the water for purity or furnish the address of some State official who will do it. Although wells may be drilled at a reasonable cost in most localities, there is always some chance that a supply of good water will not be found near the surface.

In those sections of the United States where the rainfall is scant, it may be necessary to irrigate the crops during at least a part of the growing season. Under such conditions even more attention should be given to the water supply.

The location of the land with regard to community improvements, like roads, schools, churches, and electric-power lines, should also be considered. A part of the cost of some improvements, like paving and sidewalks, is often assessed against the adjoining property. This should be considered when deciding between two tracts of land, if only one has city improvements. The amount of the tax levy for recent years and the probable future taxes should be investigated.

In many cases a small tract of land with a house and outbuildings can be bought more cheaply than it would be possible to buy unimproved land and put up the buildings. But if the chief object is to have a place to raise a supply of food for the family, the quality of the soil should have greater weight than the state of repair of the buildings. In the New England and other eastern States uncleared land on the outskirts of cities is sometimes available at a very low price. Many city people have bought small tracts for home sites, but such land requires a great deal of labor to make it productive. Moreover, care must be taken on uncleared areas to keep rodents and other small-animal pests of agriculture sufficiently under control to insure a full crop.

Small acreages near cities are available for rent. These can usually be rented with the payment of rent on a monthly basis. A year's experience in renting such a place will not only make it possible to decide for oneself on the advantages and disadvantages of living on a subsistence homestead, but it will furnish an excellent basis of judgment as to the advantages and disadvantages of the particular property as compared with some other one located nearby.

If the purchaser hopes to increase his farming later, in order to have produce for sale, he should keep the possibilities of such increase in mind when buying.

VEGETABLE, POULTRY, AND FRUIT PRODUCTION

Enough vegetables and small fruits can be raised on one half to three quarters of an acre of good land to furnish a family of five with all they want during the summer and with plenty for canned, stored, and dried products for the winter. These small fruits and vegetables, together with a small poultry flock and a few fruit trees, are all that can be cared for properly by the ordinary family without a horse or garden tractor, if the man is chiefly employed in some other job during the growing season.

LAY-OUT FOR A SMALL ACREAGE

Figures 1 and 2 give suggested plans for using approximately 1 acre of land. Figure 1 shows a plan that is suitable in the North or Northern States as far west as there is sufficient rainfall. Figure 2 shows a plan adapted to the South or the old Cotton Belt. It is to be emphasized that these plans are merely suggestive. The topography and the quality of land vary so greatly in many localities that the plan for using any plot of land must be adapted to its specific conditions.

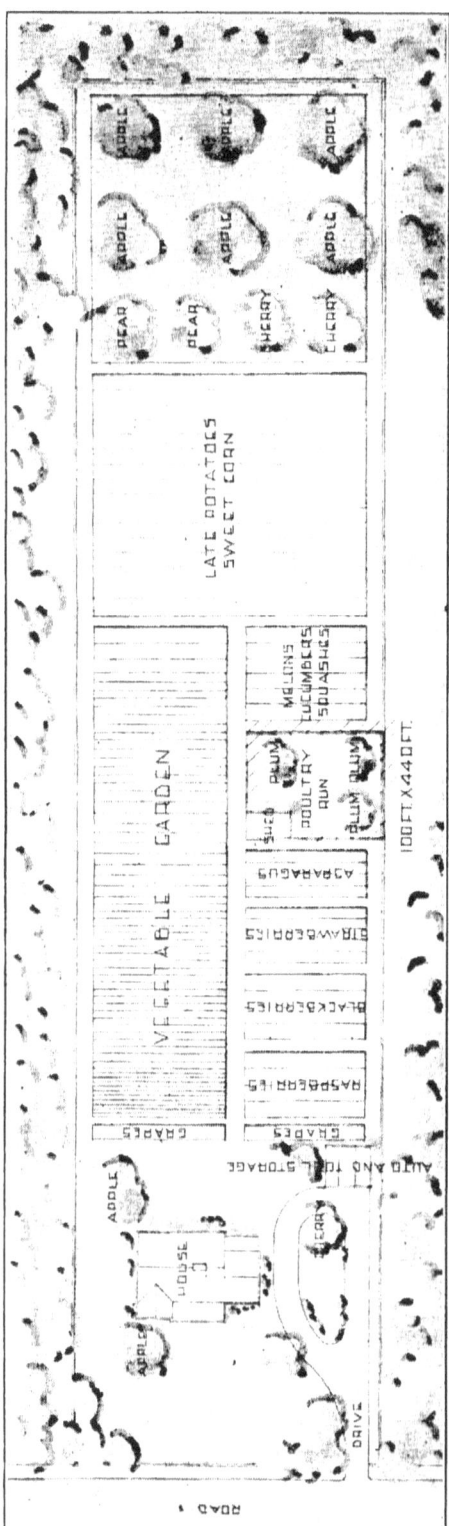

FIGURE 1.—A SUGGESTED PLAN FOR A 1-ACRE SUBSISTENCE HOMESTEAD IN THE NORTH.

Beauty and utility are combined in the lay-out of this tract containing 1.01 acres. In the area north of the Mason-Dixon line and east of the one hundredth meridian this plan provides for a year's supply of vegetables, small fruits, poultry products, early and late potatoes, and most of the necessary tree fruits for a family of five. This is all that a man who is employed elsewhere during the growing season can care for properly by hand with the help of his family.

A few important points are to be kept in mind in planning the home and grounds, regardless of locality. Although the chief object in securing a small acreage may be economy—growing food for the family and lowering the housing costs—beauty or sightliness should not be overlooked when planning the buildings, garden, and tree plantings. Success in changing from a city to a country type of living will depend more on the wife—on her ability and willingness to adapt herself to the new conditions and responsibilities—than on any other member of the family. Careful arrangement of the buildings and plantings will do much to make country living attractive to the family.

Economy of effort is important. The use of the land should be planned so that the work can be done with the least possible effort. This means that the vegetables and berries that need the most attention should be closest to the house. As more trips are made to the garden for small vegetables and berries than for late potatoes, sweet corn, and orchard fruit, the small vegetables and

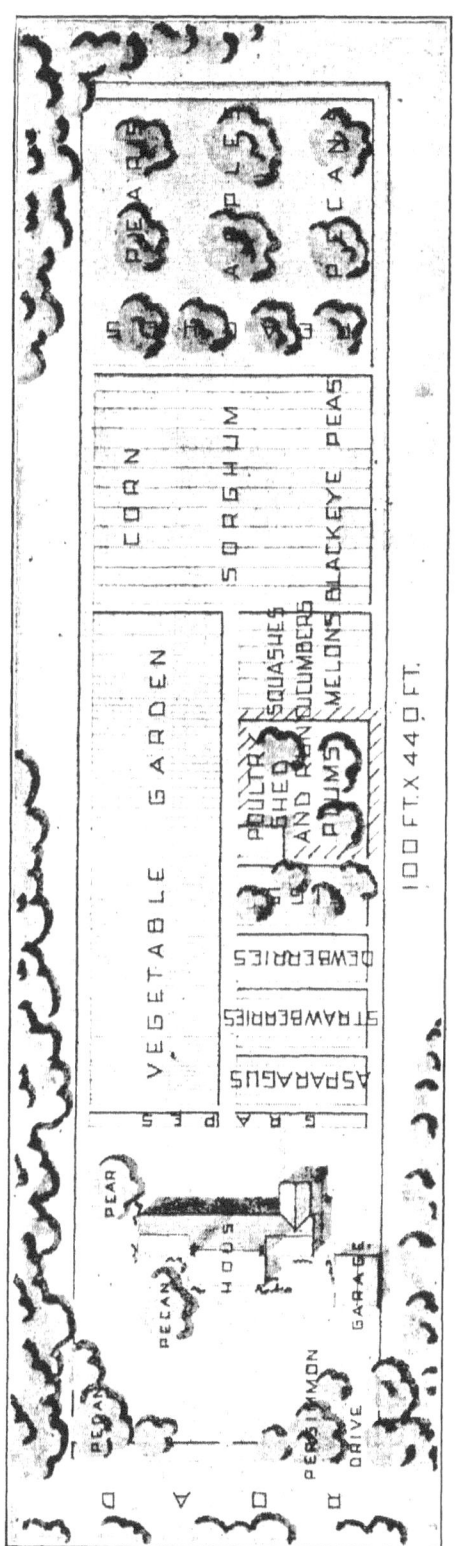

FIGURE 2.—A SUGGESTED PLAN FOR A 1-ACRE SUBSISTENCE HOMESTEAD IN THE SOUTH.
This lay-out differs from figure 1 in that it is adapted to that region of the United States often called the old Cotton Belt.

berries should be located nearer the kitchen. If the condition of the land permits, all the cultivated part should be located in one tract to facilitate the preparation of the seed beds and the cultivation. Since poultry requires attention at least twice a day, the chickens should be located reasonably near the house. Trees require the least care and, with the exception of those used for shade, should be located farthest from the house.

QUANTITY AND VARIETY OF GARDEN VEGETABLES AND SMALL FRUITS

Detailed plans for vegetable gardens in the North and South respectively are given in table 1. The amount of each vegetable crop to plant and the standard variety for the general region are suggested, as a guide for those who are not experienced. There may be other equally good or better varieties for any given locality or soil type within the region. The State agricultural experiment station and extension service or reliable garden-seed companies may be able to recommend varieties that are better adapted to specific local conditions.

To be most useful, the vegetable garden must provide a succession of crops throughout the growing season, and a supply for canning and storage for use during the other months. Varieties should be selected with these requirements in mind. With success in growing, the quantity of the various vegetables indicated in the tables will supply an adequate and balanced diet for the average family of five throughout the entire year.

Strawberries do well in most localities and bear fruit the second year after the plants are set out. Some of the better everbearing varieties will produce fruit throughout the fall of the first year. The Klondike and Missionary varieties are best for the Gulf coast region. The Southland, a new home-garden variety, is excellent for other parts of the South. Late summer or early fall is the proper time to set out strawberry plants in the South.

TABLE 1.—*Garden vegetables for a family of five*

IN THE NORTHERN STATES

Crop	Variety	50-foot rows	Succession crop	Distance between rows
		Number		*Inches*
Radishes	Scarlet Globe	1	Fall spinach	
Lettuce	New York and Simpson	1	....do....	
Onions	Japanese	2	....do....	
Beets	Detroit Dark Red	1		18
Carrots	Chantenay	2		
Swiss Chard	Lucullus	1		
Parsnips	Hollow Crown	1		
Salsify	Sandwich Island	1		
Peas	Alaska	1	Late beans	
	Little Marvel	1	....do....	
	Thos. Laxton	1	....do....	
	Telephone	2	....do....	
Snap beans	Early Bountiful	1	Late cabbage	
	Tendergreen	1	....do....	
	Currie Rust-Proof Wax	1	....do....	
	Stringless Green Pod	1	....do....	30
Lima beans	Henderson Bush	2		
	Fordhook Bush	2		
Early cabbage	Jersey Wakefield	2		
Broccoli	Italian Sprouting	1		
Early potatoes	Irish Cobbler or Triumph	8	Late cabbage	
Snap beans (2d and 3d planting)	Stringless Green Pod	2		
	Early Bountiful	2		
Tomatoes (early, staked)	Pritchard	2		
Tomatoes (not staked)	Marglobe	4		48
Early sweet corn	Golden Cross Bantam	5	Kale	
Medium sweet corn	Country Gentleman	5	Turnips	36
Late sweet corn	Stowell Evergreen	5		
Pole beans	Kentucky Wonder	1		
	Pole lima	1		42

IN THE OLD COTTON BELT

Spinach	Savoy	5	Swiss Chard	
Radishes	Scarlet Globe	1		
	White Icicle	1	Carrots	
Lettuce	White Boston	1		
	Curled Simpson	1	Beets	
Onions (sets)		2		18
Onions (plants)	Valencia	2	Fall lettuce	
Beets	Early Eclipse	1		
	Detroit Dark Red	1	Spinach	
Carrots	Chantenay	3	....do....	
Early turnips		4	....do....	
Mustard	Southern Curled	3	....do....	
Early cabbage	Charleston Wakefield	3	Late beans	
Snap beans	Early Bountiful	2	....do....	
	Stringless Black Valentine	2	....do....	
	Rustproof	2	....do....	36
Lima beans	Small bush	3		
Broccoli	Italian Sprouting	2		
Collards	Georgia	4		
Tomatoes (staked)	Marglobe	5		48
Tomatoes (not staked)	....do....	4		
Early potatoes	Irish Cobbler or Triumph	5	Late turnips (broadcast)	36
Black Eye peas		4		
Sweetpotatoes		17		42
Okra	Perkins Mammoth	2		36
Pole beans	Kentucky Wonder	2		42

From North Carolina northward to the Canadian border the Premier or Howard 17 is one of the most popular strawberry varieties. Two good new varieties, the Fairfax and the Dorsett, are also well adapted to this region. For the northern Great Plains, the Howard 17, Dunlap, and Progressive are among the most popular varieties. The Progressive is an everbearing variety.

Strawberry plants can be set out in the spring in the Northern States and, if given proper care, will yield the second year. They do well in most localities. Some of the better everbearing varieties will produce fruit throughout the fall of the first year. Fifty plants for each member of the family are often recommended as a guide for planting. The strawberry bed should be so located that it can be changed and replanted every 2 years under most conditions.

Grapes bear well in most localities and are relatively easy to care for once the proper methods of pruning and training are learned. They usually reach practically full bearing in the third year after planting. In the Northern States the Concord, Niagara, and Moore's Early are the most popular varieties. In the Southeastern States, the Thomas and Scuppernong varieties are the most popular. About 10 plants set 10 feet apart in the row are plenty for an ordinary family. Grapes require a trellis and careful pruning each year for best results.

Raspberries, blackberries, and dewberries cannot be grown successfully in as large a part of the United States as grapes and strawberries. Dewberries winter kill in the Northern States but are excellent for the South. Raspberries and blackberries do not bear well in the far South. Raspberries, blackberries, and dewberries should bear the second year after planting in those sections of the country where they do well. About 50 to 100 plants of each planted 3 to 4 feet apart in the row should furnish plenty of berries for the ordinary family.

A small asparagus bed should also be found in each family garden and in the North a few hills of rhubarb.

Only a few inexpensive tools are necessary to care for the garden and berries. A good hoe, a garden rake, a spade or spading fork, a pair of pruning shears, and a trowel are all that are essential. Much hard work can be saved if a wheel hoe with a large wheel and a well-built wheel barrow can be bought. Other tools may be useful but are not necessary.

THE SMALL POULTRY FLOCK

Most families who are interested in raising their own vegetables are also interested in producing their own poultry and eggs. Studies in several States indicate that almost all part-time farmers keep a few hens, usually not over 25. A flock of 25 hens can be kept on very little land. They are fed on table scraps and some grain, and thus furnish eggs at low cost for home use. Their manure may be used on the garden land, thus reducing fertilizer cost. A few young chickens can be raised on a different small plot of land each year, in rotation with the garden and truck patch, or on the land planted to young fruit trees. In case the latter plan is used, the young growing trees must be protected.

The necessary permanent buildings and equipment for 25 hens and 40 young chickens would cost about $50 if built with home labor. Temporary buildings made of second-hand lumber and covered with roofing paper may be built for much less. The yearly expense for purchased grain for this number of chickens would be from $25 to $40. If they are well cared for, 25 hens are more than enough to supply the family with eggs throughout the year. In addition, approximately 20 young chickens weighing 3 pounds each and 12 hens weighing 4 to 6 pounds each would be available for meat. This is about 120 pounds of meat of a kind all families like.

There are great differences in the number of eggs produced by the same number of hens under different conditions. Commercial flocks average between 12 and 14 dozen eggs per hen, each year, but the average production in the United States is less than 7 dozen. With good care and housing, the pullets in the flock will lay all winter, but the spring months naturally bring the heaviest laying. It will probably take a few years of experience to get good fall and winter egg production. Eggs are usually lowest in price during the spring and highest in price during the fall and winter. During the heavy laying season in the spring the surplus eggs can be preserved in water glass for use in the winter. On request, the county agricultural agent or the home demonstration agent will furnish, without cost, instructions regarding the use of water glass.

Unless this plan is used the first year or two, it may be necessary to buy eggs in the fall and winter. As in the case of gardening, starting in a small way in egg production is advisable for the beginner. A dozen pullets may be enough for the first year. If the family is successful in getting good egg production from this number, they will have enough fresh eggs for their own use. If good production is not obtained the first year (and this would not be unusual) a larger flock would only mean a larger feed bill.

Losses in the raising of young chickens are likely to be heavy unless the chicks are fed properly and parasites and diseases controlled. To raise only a few chickens the first year will give the needed experience and will keep down the risk of heavy losses.

PRODUCTION OF TREE FRUITS ON SMALL ACREAGES

To grow tree fruits, especially winter apples, may be doubtful economy if the land is high priced and the family has enough cash income to buy these fruits. These trees do not come into bearing for several years; peaches take about 4 years, cherries and plums 4 to 5 years, and apples 6 to 8 years. During this time they must be cared for, sprayed, and pruned if they are to yield well at maturity. A well-rounded program of production for family subsistence, however, should include cherries, plums, peaches, pears, and apples in all localities where such trees bear well.

Bearing fruit trees should be sprayed several times each year, to kill the various insects and to combat the diseases that attack the trees and the fruit. This work is often neglected by those who have only a few trees, as it requires some special equipment, but unless this need is fully realized there is likely to be disappointment later.

A barrel mounted on a 2-wheel cart and fitted with a hand sprayer can be bought or built at a cost of not more than $30. This equipment can be used to spray the trees on 5 to 10 homesteads having 10 to 15 trees each. If the spraying equipment is owned in partnership the cost would be only $3 to $6 for each family.

FERTILIZERS

If the vegetables and other crops are to be cultivated entirely by hand, the intensive use of a small piece of land with heavy fertilization is more feasible and will give better results than the use of a larger area of land in medium or poor condition. Stable or barn-lot manure, when it can be obtained at a reasonable price, is the best garden fertilizer for most soils. A first application of 20 large wagonloads of partly rotted manure on a half-acre garden is not too much, if the land is lacking in organic matter and fertility. However, such manure is usually scarce and expensive near cities. The time to apply the manure will vary, but as a rule it should be spread just before the ground is plowed.

Commercial fertilizers can be used to advantage in many cases along with the manure from the poultry flock. An application at the rate of 600 to 1,200 pounds to the acre, when no manure is available, will usually prove satisfactory. A fertilizer that contains about 5 percent of nitrogen, 10 to 20 percent of phosphoric acid (usually in the form of superphosphate), and 5 or 6 percent of potash is about right for general garden crops. After the ground has been spaded or plowed, the fertilizer should be worked into the ground before the vegetables or other crops are planted.

INSECTS, DISEASES, AND OTHER HANDICAPS

Diseases, insects, rodents, and other pests attack the vegetables as well as the fruits and poultry. These pests, or poor seed, or unfavorable weather may cause a partial or total failure of any one crop or planting. Several plantings help to insure against total loss. A safe plan for the inexperienced is to plant only a small amount of each crop the first year or two. On the basis of the experience thus gained the family can decide which crops are the best for them, considering both what they are successful with and what the family needs.

Even if the first efforts are not successful, the particular crop or variety need not be condemned. Perhaps neighbors have been very successful with it. If so, it probably can be grown successfully if the right methods are used. The county agricultural agent, usually located at the county seat, will be able to give information on all such subjects without cost to the farmers. State agricultural experiment stations will send free bulletins about vegetable growing, insects and diseases, poultry raising, and other agricultural problems, on request. A list of free bulletins published by the Government, which are likely to be of interest to subsistence-homesteaders will be found on page 19.

CASH EXPENSES FOR AGRICULTURAL PRODUCTION AND RETURNS

Cash operating expenses in connection with such a program as outlined in the suggested 1-acre plan would be about as follows:

1 man and team—plowing and preparing the seed bed in the spring (5 hours)	$2.50 to $4
Seeds, plants, and bushes (after first year)	3.00 to 5
Fertilizer (300 to 600 pounds)	4.50 to 9
Insecticides	3.00 to 6
Feed for chickens (1,600 to 2,000 pounds of grain)	25.00 to 40
Total	38.00 to 64

The careful manager can sometimes reduce these cash outlays by exchanging tools with neighbors, by trading work, or by promising to trade products at the end of the season for items obtained earlier.

In return for the family's investment in the land, and its labor and cash expenses for the season, as indicated above, the family will get most of its supply of vegetables for the year, its entire supply of eggs and poultry for the year, and most of its fruit. The value of these vegetables and fruits has been variously estimated at from $70 to $150. If the 25 hens average 8 dozen eggs apiece, valued at 20 cents a dozen, the total value of the eggs produced would be $40; and 120 pounds of poultry meat at 25 cents a pound would be $30. This means that the total value of food from the 1-acre tract would be from $140 to $220.

It might be pointed out that an adequate diet at moderate cost for a very active family of five, as worked out by the United States Bureau of Home Economics, calls for only 85 dozen eggs. This indicates that about 100 dozen eggs would be available for sale if 25 hens are kept, but it would be at the season when egg prices are low, unless unusually progressive poultry practices are used.

WINTER VEGETABLE AND FRUIT SUPPLY FOR A FAMILY OF FIVE

The gardens and fruit trees suggested in the planting diagrams should provide ample supplies for use during the growing season, and also a generous quantity for winter needs. In the North fresh foods will be available for about 4 or 5 months. The southern gardens will produce during a longer period, although in some sections little can be grown during the hot, dry, midsummer months. Early in the year the family should make an estimate of the quantities of the various foods to be stored, canned, and otherwise preserved for use during the nonproductive months. The best method to use will depend upon the crops raised, the climate, and other local conditions.

Storing in cellars or pits is practicable for such relatively nonperishable crops as potatoes, carrots, beets, turnips, parsnips, onions, cabbage, apples, and pears. Sweetpotatoes, after a first curing, must be kept in a dry, warm, well-ventilated place; squash and pumpkin should also be stored in a dry, warm place.

Drying may be used to keep beans, peas, okra, corn, squash, and some fruits; 1 to 2 bushels of dried beans and peas and 15 to 30 pounds of dried fruit is a generous winter supply for a family of five.

Canning, in either glass jars or tin cans, is the best method of preservation for some foods. If proper equipment for canning cannot be bought by single families it may be possible to establish a community canning center where the equipment can be used cooperatively. The Department of Agriculture at Washington, D.C. will send a mimeographed leaflet on community canning centers, on request. A pressure cooker should be used for canning such vegetables as leafy greens, asparagus, beans, peas, okra, corn, or root vegetables. Unless a pressure cooker is available it is advisable to limit the canning to fruits, rhubarb, and acid vegetables, such as tomatoes, tomato combinations, sauerkraut, and beets in vinegar.

The two canning budgets that follow are suggested as general guides for families living in the North and South, respectively. More detailed canning plans based on the conditions peculiar to the individual States can be obtained from the extension services of the various State agricultural colleges or from the local home demonstration agent. The quantities suggested in the following budgets will provide 2 or 3 one-half-cup servings of canned fruits or vegetables for each member of the family for each day of the months when the garden is not producing. Used in connection with the stored and dried products, this amount of canned foods should be enough to meet the usual needs of a family of five. But it might be well to allow an additional 10 to 15 percent to care for guests, spoilage, or emergencies such as poor crops during the following season. As most properly canned food will keep well for at least 2 years, any that is unused may be carried over to use during the second year. It is best not to hold canned foods for longer than 2 years.

During the first few years a new homestead plot may not furnish enough fruit to supply the quantities suggested in the canning budgets. In some sections there may be wild fruits and berries to use. If enough fruit cannot be obtained, the quantities of the various canned vegetables should be increased somewhat.

Fruit and vegetable canning budget for family of five in the Northern States

[For use during 7 nonproductive months]

Tomatoes	quarts	100 to 150
Leafy greens (spinach, chard, etc.)	do	20 to 35
Other green vegetables (asparagus, string or lima beans, peas, okra, etc.)	quarts	20 to 35
Sauerkraut	do	15 to 20
Sweet corn	do	15 to 20
Soup mixtures	do	10 to 20
Fruits (peaches, pears, quinces, plums, grapes, cherries, berries, apples, apple sauce, etc.)	quarts	90 to 130
Fruit juices	do	15 to 25
Catsup, pickles, chow-chow, etc	pints	15 to 25
Jellies, jams, fruit butters, etc	do	15 to 25

Fruit and vegetable canning budget for family of five in the Southern States

[For use during 6 nonproductive months]

Tomatoes (if citrus fruits are available the quantity of canned tomatoes may be reduced)	quarts	75 to 125
Leafy greens (fresh greens are available for 12 months in many southern localities).		
Other green vegetables (asparagus, string or lima beans, peas, okra, etc.)	quarts	20 to 40
Sweet corn	do	15 to 25
Soup mixtures	do	15 to 25

Sauerkraut	quarts	10 to 15
Carrots and other vegetables	do	10 to 15
Fruits (peaches, pears, plums, figs, grapes, berries, cherries, etc.)	quarts	75 to 110
Fruit juices	do	15 to 25
Catsup, pickles, chow-chow, etc	pints	15 to 25
Jellies, jams, fruit butters, etc	do	15 to 25

FEED AND LIVESTOCK PRODUCTION ON A SUBSISTENCE HOMESTEAD

If horse or mechanical power is available at a reasonable cost the farm plans can be materially changed to advantage. The garden and truck patch may be laid out in long rows, 3 feet apart, and can be cultivated with power throughout the growing season. This will greatly reduce the hand labor and will permit the use of a larger acreage.

Figure 3 shows a suggested plan for fruit and vegetable production where power is available. Approximately 2 acres of land are included in this plan. Unless some arrangement can be made to secure power cultivation at reasonable cost this plan will not be feasible. To keep a horse or garden tractor for use on such a small piece of cultivated land is questionable economy. A half-acre orchard may not be considered desirable since fruit cannot be gathered for several years. In that case the ground might be used to grow corn or other feed crops for the poultry.

If an orchard is planted as indicated, during the first few years while the trees are young, many of the garden vegetables can be raised in the space between the trees. This would leave some of the other land for growing feed for the poultry.

The one fourth acre sown to legumes in figure 3, if planted to the appropriate crops, may be used in growing the young chickens.

THE FAMILY COW

Studies indicate that a family of five should have from 1,200 to 1,500 quarts of milk and 90 to 150 pounds of butter a year. One good cow can supply these needs most of the time. From the standpoint of an adequate diet for children in families that have very low incomes, keeping a cow would seem to be more valuable than raising vegetables or fruits. But the keeping of a cow by inexperienced people, on a small piece of land has many disadvantages which may make it questionable.

A high-producing dairy cow is a sensitive animal, responding to good care, but quick to give less milk on receiving poor or improper care. Milking, feeding, and watering require regular attention twice each day. But if a family is willing to undertake the regular care of a cow and has a natural knack for taking care of animals it should have no serious difficulties in obtaining a reasonably satisfactory quantity of milk.

Although one good cow, well cared for, will give over 7,000 pounds of milk (the quantity necessary to supply the milk and butter for the family of five), the average production in the United States is only about 4,500 pounds per cow. As the usual lactation period for a cow is 10 or 11 months, at best, milk and butter would have to be bought during part of the year. It is reasonable to estimate that, with ordi-

PLANNING A SUBSISTENCE HOMESTEAD 13

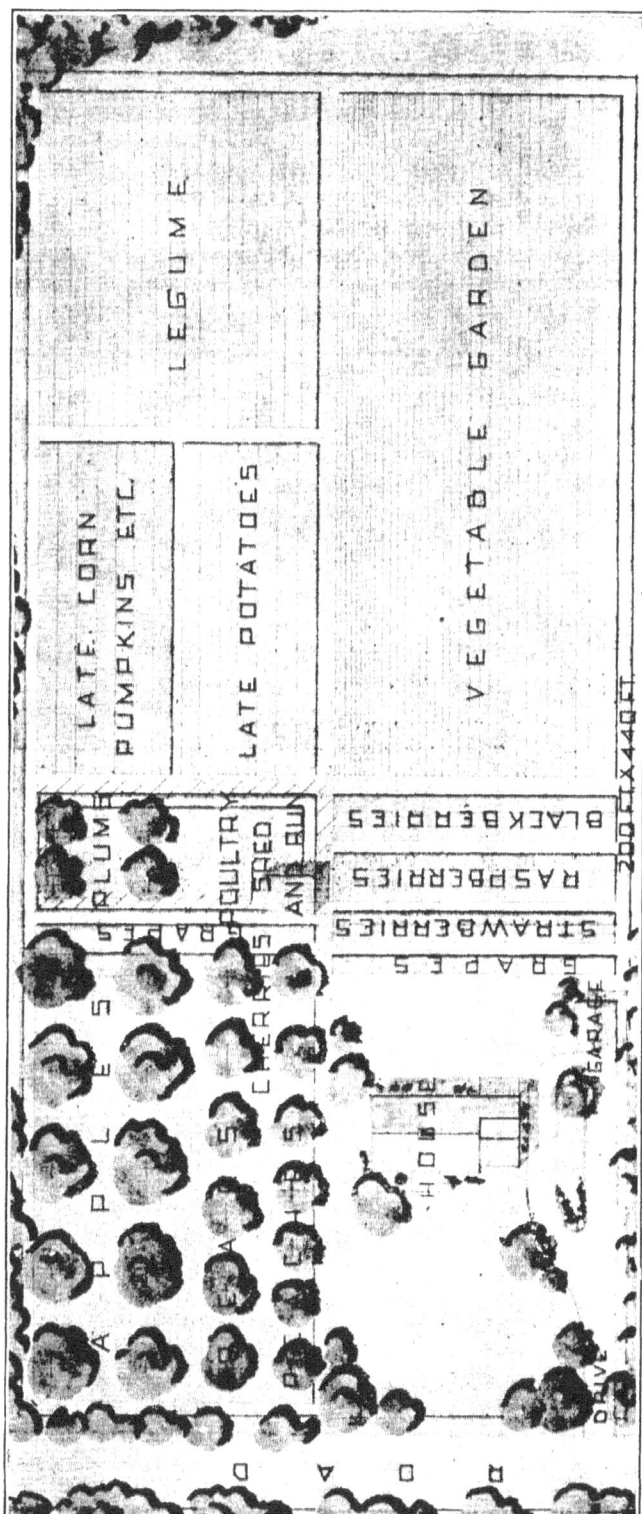

FIGURE 3.—A SUGGESTED PLAN FOR A 2-ACRE SUBSISTENCE HOMESTEAD

Cultivation with horse or tractor power requires wider rows and a larger garden. It also makes it possible to care for a larger acreage. Alternate uses of the space allotted for an orchard and for the rotation of crops are: as pasture for a cow, pasture for milk goats, or pasture for pigs, or for the growing of feed grains for poultry.

nary care, a cow will furnish both the milk and butter for a family of five for 4 months of the year. For another 6 or 7 months there will be plenty of milk, but the butter will have to be bought. Both milk and butter would have to be bought for the remaining 1 or 2 months. If a cow is kept, it may be more economical to sell the extra milk to neighbors and buy butter, rather than try to make butter. The money from sales of milk at retail prices during the first part of the lactation period would not only buy the butter during this period but would largely pay for the necessary purchases of milk during the period when the cow is dry. The question of whether or not to keep a cow may turn on the possibility of selling the extra milk to neighbors at retail prices.

In the Northeastern and Midwestern States, 1 to 2 acres are necessary to pasture a cow. If the land on a 2-acre tract is very productive and no orchard is wanted, enough pasture and green crops could be grown to feed a cow during the summer. A better balanced plan of farm production for family subsistence purposes, however, would be attained by adding 2 acres of pasture to the 2-acre plot suggested above. Figure 4 shows how this might be done, with the pasture arranged so that the cow will come up close to the house for watering, feeding, and milking.

Good summer pasture, supplemented by roughage from the garden, will reduce to a minimum the grain to be fed to the dairy cow during summer months. During the winter in the Northern States a cow will need about 2½ tons of hay, costing from $20 to $38, and from 1,000 to 2,000 pounds of grain, costing from $10 to $30. A shed, built in connection with the poultry house or some other outbuilding, large enough to keep a cow and some feed would cost from $50 to $150. In the South the milder climate makes a warm building unnecessary, but some form of shelter should be provided even there.

MILK GOATS

If for any reason a cow will not be kept, milk goats might be considered in those communities where breeding stock is available. In the southwestern and western parts of the United States in particular, a number of the families on small acreages keep a milk goat or two to supply milk for the family. An ordinary milk goat gives from 1½ to 2 quarts of milk a day and needs only about one sixth as much feed as a cow. Three to five does would be necessary to furnish an ample supply of milk throughout the year for a family of five.

There are a number of things to be learned before buying a milk goat. Farmers' Bulletin 920 on milk goats gives some valuable general information and will be sent free by the United States Department of Agriculture on request. In general, people in this country do not know much about milk goats, but in some communities there may be neighbors who have had experience in keeping goats who can give advice and information.

PORK FOR FAMILY USE

A family of five requires from 400 to 600 pounds of meats and cooking fat a year. This quantity can be produced in the form of pork and lard by growing and fattening three pigs. But most

PLANNING A SUBSISTENCE HOMESTEAD 15

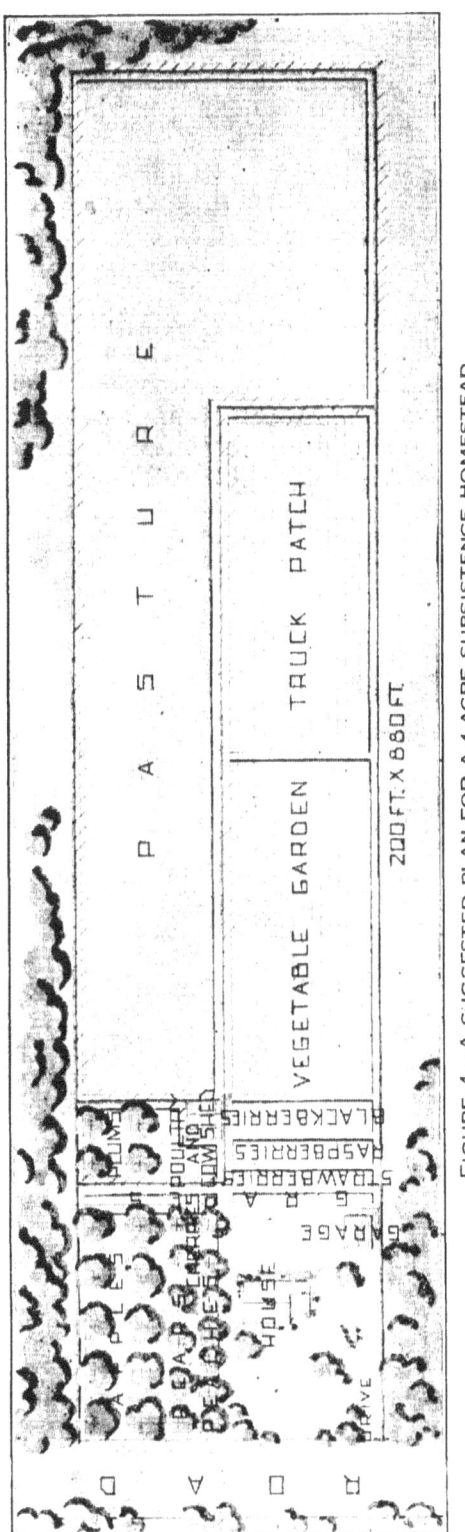

FIGURE 4.—A SUGGESTED PLAN FOR A 4-ACRE SUBSISTENCE HOMESTEAD

The addition of 2 acres of pasture to the plan suggested in figure 3 will provide ample pasture for a cow in those sections of the United States where grass grows well.

families will not wish to depend on hogs alone for their meat, even though they also have eggs and poultry from their own flock.

In some States and communities there are regulations that prohibit the raising of pigs close to neighbors. In any case, pigs should be kept some distance from any house, even though water and feed must be carried to them.

Two or three pigs can be kept in a small pen and fed table scraps and some grain. Thus they grow into 500 to 700 pounds of live pork at a relatively low cost if the grain can be raised or bought economically. Pigs can be bought as weanlings in most communities for from $3 to $5 each. Pigs immunized against cholera should be bought, particularly if table scraps are to be fed. A pig will eat from 600 to 1,000 pounds of grain costing $6 to $15, while growing to a weight of 200 pounds. Savings of 10 to 20 percent on feed costs may be expected if one fourth to one half of an acre of good pasture can be provided. Shade is very important for pigs in the summer. Plenty of fresh water is also essential. A comparison of the cost of small pigs plus the cost of grain for feed on the one hand and the price of dressed pork on the other, should be made. This, and the effort and risk involved, should be considered carefully before a decision is made. Studies of part-time farmers show that only one fourth to one third of these men (mostly on the larger acreages) keep cows and even fewer keep pigs. Evidently most of them find it more economical or easier to buy their milk and meat.

Manure from the animals is valuable for the garden and reduces the cash expenses for fertilizer. Much of the cow manure would be used on the pasture; but even so, fertilizer requirements for the cultivated land should be reduced by 50 to 70 percent when 25 hens, a cow, and pigs are kept.

FEED FOR LIVESTOCK ON SMALL ACREAGES

Many people who want to raise as much of the family's food supply as possible with the lowest cash cost, plan to keep poultry, a cow or two, and pigs, and to raise the necessary feeds. It takes about 1½ acres of land to raise the necessary corn and wheat for 25 hens and 40 young chickens. In addition to 2 acres of pasture for a cow, approximately 1¾ acres are necessary to raise the hay and 1¼ acres to raise the grain consumed by the cow during the year. This makes a total of 5 acres for one cow; if two cows are kept this acreage should be doubled. One and one half acres should produce enough grain to fatten three pigs.

Using 6 acres of land for raising feed in addition to 1 acre of garden and truck crops would require the work of a man and team 15 to 25 days during the growing and harvesting season. If a one-horse outfit were used, 30 to 50 days would be required. This is too small an amount of work for one horse if the overhead cost is to be kept low. On the other hand, to hire a man and team 15 to 25 days at the usual rates means a considerable cash expense.

A horse requires about the same quantity of feed and pasture as a cow. If a horse is to be kept, 5 more acres should be obtained. It might be possible for two or more families to own a horse or team in partnership and thus reduce the cost.

Therefore, if a family plans to do the work by hand an intensive use of a relatively small piece of land will probably be more satisfactory than spreading the effort over a larger area. Unless a cow or pigs are kept, 1 acre of good land is enough under such circumstances. If a cow is kept and it is planned to buy the winter roughage and grain, 2 additional acres of good pasture land would be enough. A man employed elsewhere, working only a few hours a day on his place during the growing season, with the help of his family can care for the vegetable garden, small fruits, a few fruit trees, and a cow without any difficulty.

If mechanical power or horsepower is available at low cost, the vegetables can be grown in wider rows and cultivated with a horse or garden tractor. This makes it possible to put to good use a larger acreage. But it is difficult to have horse cultivation at low cost on a very small acreage. Large families with small incomes, who have considerable free time during the growing season may find it economical to keep a horse, 1 or 2 cows, and some pigs, and raise the farm-grown feeds for the livestock in addition to the vegetables and fruits. At least 15 acres of good land should be acquired in such cases. A careful study should be made of all sides of the question before a family decides to undertake so much farm work for family living purposes. Growing feeds on the farm in such small quantities and the cost of keeping a horse when it is used only a small part of the time mean relatively high costs and low net returns, as compared with the returns from industrial employment, if that is available.

POSSIBILITIES OF A SMALL WOOD LOT

The yearly fuel bill is always difficult for families with small incomes. More fuel is used in country homes where there is no gas or electricity for cooking. If land can be obtained which includes a few wooded acres, the family's wood supply can be provided with almost no additional cash cost. Cutting can be done in the winter or whenever there is extra time, and if the trees to be cut are carefully selected, the supply of timber will continue throughout the owner's lifetime. Perhaps some exchange of work could be arranged with an owner of a team, in order to have the wood hauled to the house.

If the farmer does not buy any timberland but there is considerable timber in the community, he may be able to get the privilege of cutting his fuel supply from a neighbor's woods for a very small sum.

LIMITATIONS OF SMALL ACREAGES AS A MEANS OF SELF-SUPPORT

Letters coming from townspeople show that more often they hear about the best results from farming than about the poorest results; it has therefore seemed best to caution the reader frequently not to regard subsistence farming too optimistically. No real service is rendered in holding out rosy possibilities when the probabilities are slight that such results will be realized by most people. On the other hand it is not intended to discourage those townspeople who are handicapped by lack of capital and are getting only a small income, if they have an honest wish to better their conditions by raising most of their food supply even though it means some trouble and much work.

The work may be hard and the results not always up to expectations; but if the family has no better possibility almost any arrangement to obtain the use of a piece of land should be better than continued idleness or full support from charity or relief funds.

It cannot be overemphasized, however, that a program of farm production as here outlined, even though all the livestock feed is raised, does not make the family self-maintaining. Cash farm expenses must be met, such as the purchase of seeds and feeds that cannot be raised economically, taxes, and repairs of equipment. Family living expenses for clothes, school supplies, and medical care mean cash expenditures. Part-time farming studies do not throw much light on the minimum cash income necessary to meet these expenses. The average cash income reported for those groups of part-time farmers whose financial relations were studied varied from $400 to $900 in most cases.

A number of people, after gaining farm experience, will find that they can raise some products for sale at a profit. A commercial poultry business large enough to employ a man full time and bring in an adequate income can be developed on as little as 2 acres if conditions are right.

PRODUCTION FOR HOME USE ON LARGER ACREAGES

Many people in towns who have little hope of further employment, because of age or for other reasons, would like to get a larger acreage of cheap land on which they can become independent for the rest of their lives. They are chiefly interested in producing for home use; they are interested in producing for sale only enough to furnish the few necessities of life not obtained on the farm. Usually their capital and experience are so limited that cheapness of land is their chief concern. They are naturally attracted by advertisements describing farms that can be bought for a fraction of the cost of the improvements on them.

As a matter of fact, a great deal of farm land in the United States is not productive enough to be of value in growing market crops and livestock. This is especially true in the southern Appalachian region, the Ozarks, the New England States, and the cut-over areas of the Southern and Great Lake States. Many farms in these areas have very low producing possibilities, and the families on them grow crops and livestock almost entirely for their own use.

SELF-SUFFICING FARMS

The 1930 agricultural census, in its study of types of farming, classified all farms as self-sufficing where 50 percent or more of the value of the farm products was consumed by the family. This group of farms, 498,019 in 1929, compares with the type of farming many townspeople propose to engage in. These self-sufficing farms are most common in the southern Appalachian region. Figures from a study of 151,000 of these self-sufficing farms in this region show how meager a living those people really had.

Most of the farms were from 20 to 100 acres in size. The average value was $2,029. The value of tools and machinery per farm was only $74. Not all of the farms had horses; only a little over one half of them kept milk cows; and about one half of them kept hogs. The total value of the farm products sold, traded, or used by the operator's family, in 1929, was $464, of which $323 was used by the operator's family.

INDIVIDUAL FARMS VARY IN PRODUCTIVITY

Studies indicate that the opportunities or likelihood of making a living on some of the farms in these poorer areas is very limited. A full set of buildings is no indication of a productive farm. Many abandoned farms, several hundred acres in size, have failed to yield a reasonable living under any type of farming. Many families living in these areas have another source of income, such as cutting wood for sale, road work, or coal mining, which supplements their living obtained from the farm.

Natural productivity of the soil varies greatly. To the inexperienced, good and poor soils in these regions look alike. The county agricultural agent located at the county seat will be able to appraise the relative productivity of the various farms in his county. Neighbors who have lived in the community for years should be consulted. Inquiry as to how they are farming and the results they are obtaining on their own farms, as well as the results to be expected on nearby farms for sale, may bring valuable information.

Social considerations should form an important part in making a decision. Good schools and churches and desirable associates for the growing children are always considered by responsible parents when buying a home whether in town or country. In general, the communities on poor land are not likely to be able to have good schools and churches. If there are no growing children in the family less consideration need be given this question, and if money is extremely limited it may be impossible to do much about it. But these social problems should not be overlooked.

Buying a farm entirely by correspondence is especially full of dangers. A thorough investigation before buying in unfamiliar areas will prevent many mistakes. Renting for a time before buying gives a family a chance to learn the advantages and disadvantages of any particular farm.

FARMERS' BULLETINS OF INTEREST

The following Farmers' Bulletins published by the United States Department of Agriculture deal with many of the problems encountered in agricultural production for family subsistence purposes. They are available for distribution on request.

- F.B. 1673. The Farm Garden.
- F.B. 1371. Diseases and Insects of Garden Vegetables.
- F.B. 1508. Poultry Keeping in Back Yards.
- F.B. 1652. Diseases and Parasites of Poultry.
- F.B. 1610. Dairy Farming for Beginners.
- F.B. 920. Milk Goats.
- F.B. 879. Home Storage of Vegetables.
- F.B. 1088. Selecting a Farm.
- F.B. 1746. Subsistence Farm Gardens.
- F.B. 1753. Livestock on Small Farms.
- F.B. 1762 Home Canning of Fruits, Vegetables, and Meats.
- F.B. 1800. Home-made Jellies, Jams, and Preserves.

ORGANIZATION OF THE UNITED STATES DEPARTMENT OF AGRICULTURE WHEN THIS PUBLICATION WAS LAST PRINTED

Secretary of Agriculture	HENRY A. WALLACE.
Under Secretary	CLAUDE R. WICKARD.
Assistant Secretary	GROVER B. HILL.
Director of Information	M. S. EISENHOWER.
Director of Extension Work	M. L. WILSON.
Director of Finance	W. A. JUMP.
Director of Personnel	ROY F. HENDRICKSON.
Director of Research	JAMES T. JARDINE.
Director of Marketing	MILO R. PERKINS.
Solicitor	MASTIN G. WHITE.
Land Use Coordinator	M. S. EISENHOWER.
Office of Plant and Operations	ARTHUR B. THATCHER, Chief.
Office of C. C. C. Activities	FRED W. MORRELL, Chief.
Office of Experiment Stations	JAMES T. JARDINE, Chief.
Office of Foreign Agricultural Relations	LESLIE A. WHEELER, Director.
Agricultural Adjustment Administration	R. M. EVANS, Administrator.
Bureau of Agricultural Chemistry and Engineering.	HENRY G. KNIGHT, Chief.
Bureau of Agricultural Economics	H. R. TOLLEY, Chief.
Agricultural Marketing Service	C. W. KITCHEN, Chief.
Bureau of Animal Industry	JOHN R. MOHLER, Chief.
Commodity Credit Corporation	CARL B. ROBBINS, President.
Commodity Exchange Administration	J. W. T. DUVEL, Chief.
Bureau of Dairy Industry	O. E. REED, Chief.
Bureau of Entomology and Plant Quarantine	LEE A. STRONG, Chief.
Farm Credit Administration	A. G. BLACK, Governor.
Farm Security Administration	W. W. ALEXANDER, Administrator.
Federal Crop Insurance Corporation	LEROY K. SMITH, Manager.
Federal Surplus Commodities Corporation	MILO R. PERKINS, President.
Food and Drug Administration	WALTER G. CAMPBELL, Chief.
Forest Service	EARLE H. CLAPP, Acting Chief.
Bureau of Home Economics	LOUISE STANLEY. Chief.
Library	CLARIBEL R. BARNETT, Librarian.
Division of Marketing and Marketing Agreements.	MILO R. PERKINS, In Charge.
Bureau of Plant Industry	E. C. AUCHTER, Chief.
Rural Electrification Administration	HARRY SLATTERY, Administrator.
Soil Conservation Service	H. H. BENNETT, Chief.
Weather Bureau	FRANCIS W. REICHELDERFER, Chief.

www.ingramcontent.com/pod-product-compliance
Lightning Source LLC
Chambersburg PA
CBHW031116080526
44587CB00011B/993